# THIS IS THE YEAR

Challenges Won't Stop Me,
No More Excuse, Break Through
& Self-Focus Book

**Another Level**

# Table of Contents

# Introduction

Have you ever felt like going in circles in your life without any achievement? If you ever feel like it, look back to the last time you successfully challenged yourself. It doesn't matter if it is a tiny challenge that takes minutes to complete or a massive one that takes a year to accomplish. Bring back your memories of the last time you challenged yourself.

Do not only focus on bigger challenges! Each challenge serves a distinct purpose in terms of self-development. Each challenge needs a strong sense of self-consciousness and self-determination to let you grow as a person. It takes you out of your comfort zone, even for simple challenges like waking up early or shaking bad habits.

Meanwhile, another complex challenge will take you further from your comfort zone. Every challenge you take has its own experience, and everyone's experience is different and valuable. That is the beauty of taking on a challenge, even the simplest and tiniest one, as it opens you up to new experiences, requires you to put in the work to develop yourself every day, and enables you to really focus on yourself.

Imagine your life if you have not challenged yourself at all! You wouldn't seize any chance to enhance your talents, find a job that makes you happier, or start a new habit. Moreover, you will remain forever stuck in the box that you have built, separating you from new experiences and failures.

Do not worry about failing! Failure is not a step backward; it is a great steppingstone to success. If you can't get over your fear of failing, you'll never learn to step outside of your comfort zone. When you challenge yourself, failure is almost certain to follow, but that is natural. You will continue to fail, but what matters is how you choose to respond to those failures. You can either let that failure discourage you from trying new challenges and experiences, or you can use it as a steppingstone for new experiences and challenges.

If you've failed, now is the time to try again. If you've succeeded, it is now time for a slightly harder challenge out there. The progressive challenge manipulates you to force greater improvements in many areas, including physical, financial, emotional, and social well-being. If you want a muscular body, you must do exercises with increasing difficulty. Thus, this book helps you face challenges with a more positive and rather exciting mindset.

Once you've decided to take on a challenge, it's important to think about where to begin. Challenges come in various sizes, forms, and categories and can have an impact on your personal and professional life or both at the same time. Nowadays, we are crowded with all the social media, entertainment, and daily jobs. They most likely decrease our focus on ourselves and take the time to look at ourselves, whereas it is essential to see what is going on with our lives and what we want to achieve later in life.

Afterall, there is no gain without pain. Taking on challenges is the pain we all need so that we will doubt ourselves and the meaning of life, but eventually we can see that we can do so much more, even without this and that. It is the attitude and mentality that I want all of you to improve.

As a result, in this book, I've prepared 52 topics and 52 challenges that can be completed ideally one per week. Transform yourself in a year, and it starts right now!

# Chapter 1:

# Stop Hitting the Snooze

Snooze. Sleep. Repeat.

How often do you snooze when your alarm starts ringing? Do you have a habit of pressing the snooze button every morning? If you've often done it, you are part of the 57% who are considered habitual alarm snoozers (Mattingly et al., 2022). While snoozing can provide a few minutes of sweet relief in the early morning hours, it can also have several negative effects. This is due to snoozing, which does not result in productive sleep but rather an interrupted sleep that contributes to a groggy and tired feeling when waking up—called sleep inertia.

Sleep inertia is the temporary state between being asleep and being awake, which has effects on the slower speed of thinking and reasoning. Once repeated alarms disturb our sleep, it most likely increases the likelihood of sleep inertia compared to natural wakeup which makes you less rested even after sufficient sleep duration (Mattingly et al., 2022). Besides not feeling alert after sleep, hitting the snooze button can invoke a stress response and is not the best way for our minds to begin the day.

In contrast, having sufficient and uninterrupted sleep without hitting the snooze allows you to have a stress-free morning as you aren't rushing through your day with a calm and composed mind. As you have a better quality of sleep, you will have more energy daily. A sense of order in life comes from having a good sleep, which can also make you happier and more positive. Not only throughout the day, but early risers also tend to fall asleep faster as their bodies feel tired earlier leading to better sleep quality.

Hitting the snooze button now and then probably isn't a huge deal, but you need to challenge yourself to break these habits if you are a chronic snoozer. First, starting with the old trick of moving your alarm across the room might help physically force you to get up. Then, you need to start making a proper sleeping routine by going to bed around the same time every night and keeping your bedroom quiet, dark, and cool. One way to break the habit of snoozing at the alarm clock is to set your alarm for the time you need to wake up. This is the first step in creating a morning routine without snoozing.

In the morning, making a simple posture change after the alarm goes off will help wake up your body and avoid going back to sleep. Exposing yourself to the sunlight can also help to bring your body into a more alert state. If you already wake up in an alert state, your first activity in the morning is also essential. You may find yourself immediately scrolling on your phone before continuing your day, which often wastes your time. Thus, the next challenge will focus on reducing scrolling time on your phone.

### Challenge 1—Stop Hitting the Snooze

Now that you know the benefits of early risers and tips to stop snoozing, it's time to challenge yourself to do this challenge throughout the whole week by incorporating the tips into your morning routine to have a productive day ahead. This is neither an overnight process nor an easy one, but you will eventually carve your way out of being a habitual snoozer. If you have successfully woken up without snoozing, another extra challenge is that you need to wake up 10 minutes earlier each day.

# Chapter 2:

# Stop Scrolling

Most people lose their mornings or a significant chunk of them to endless scrolling on phones, especially social media. Most of them may start scrolling mindlessly after waking up to an alarm set on their phone with endless notifications waiting to be opened. Before you know it, it is easy for you to get sucked in, even before getting out of bed. Is this morning routine familiar to you? It might be one of the most typical morning routines for most people in this modern era.

Scrolling through social media while waking up, on the other hand, is the worst way to start the day. How many of you out there feel guilty after scrolling on your phones just moments after waking up? At first, you might only want to check your email and see the latest news, but it often leads to scrolling through social media. Despite helping you to be more productive, phones are also a major source of distraction and stress, especially when you check them first thing in the morning.

Upon waking in the morning, the brain transitions from delta waves to theta waves, which are associated with a daydreamy state. When you check your phone immediately, you are skipping the middle stage, the theta wave state, and jumping right to the alpha waves, which in fact prepare your brain for distraction (Rai, 2021). Moreover, social media often displays numerous negative news stories. The first thing you see or read in the morning, let alone the negative ones, can set off your stress response and make you anxious for the rest of the day.

Aside from negative news, you may find yourself frequently drowning in the scrolling of your friends' or even celebrities' accounts. Although it can potentially inspire you throughout the day, you can easily become overwhelmed by it and begin comparing their success to your own. In the morning, you are in the most alert state during the day, so why would you bother yourself by giving attention to other people's not-so-realistic photos and posts on social media? It only leads to harmful comparisons first thing in the morning, which wastes a lot of your precious time.

When you first open your eyes in the morning, your imaginative mind is at its peak, so you should make use of this prime time to prepare your day mindfully. To avoid scrolling your phone immediately in the morning, you can put your phone on airplane mode, so you won't be greeted with messages or notifications right when you wake up. Then, you should create another rewarding and constructive morning routine to ensure that you aren't slipping back into using your phone first thing.

There are various activities that you can replace, including exercising, spending time with family before working, listening to a podcast or music, or making coffee. In contrast to mindlessly checking your phone, engaging in these activities can reduce stress, improve attention and productivity, and clear your mind.

As soon as you turn off your alarm tomorrow, visualize the things you want to happen and the things you want to do for the day to get yourself in a better frame of mind. Remember, the way you start the day determines the tone of the day! One of the most practical and beneficial ways to do it in the morning after waking up is to tidy your place. On the next challenge, you might discover that cleaning your house is beneficial for reasons other than hygiene.

### Challenge 2—Stop Scrolling

To mindfully start this challenge on the right path, I want you to time yourself and limit it to under 10 minutes every time you start scrolling. Then, you need to reduce the scrolling time by one more minute every day. At the end of the week, you will find yourself only scrolling your phone for less than 5 minutes in the morning. For the extra challenge, do not scroll your phone at all after waking up! This habit will undoubtedly transform your morning routine into a more contented and happier one.

# Chapter 3:

# Tidy Your Place

How many times have we come home and just tossed things here and there, only to return later and tidy them up ourselves? How long did it take for you to get back in touch with them? Maybe hours? Maybe days? Maybe you are too tired, so you decided to throw your shirt, pants, dress, and socks randomly? Tell me, in the end, who is picking them up? Even after we feel stressed about it, we often repeat it again and again for the next month or maybe years.

Let's face it: keeping a tidy home takes time, effort, and continuous commitment, which can be seriously overwhelming. Sometimes, it feels easier to let the dishes pile up in the sink, the laundry lies on the floor till you have nothing to wear, or drinks roam free on the dining table. What if I told you that keeping your room or even your entire home tidy can significantly improve your overall quality of life? Have you ever noticed that it is much easier to relax in a neat place?

A house full of clutter can be a major distraction, especially if you work from home. It will be difficult for you to concentrate in a messy place, which significantly reduces your productivity while increasing error and accuracy in working activities (Mateo et al., 2013). Aside from working activities, a home is where you can take a rest and run away from the chaotic world outside. After a long day of work, it is essential to have a comfortable place to put your feet up and unwind. Maintaining a clean and organized home can create a welcoming and positive environment that you enjoy coming home to. Then, you will also be more comfortable inviting friends or family over to a tidy place.

Another essential benefit of keeping a place tidy is providing a healthy living space for you and your family. The accumulation of bacteria, dust, and other allergens in a dirty and messy place has been linked to a wide range of health issues. So, by keeping your house as neat and clean as possible, you can potentially reduce your risk of various health issues and improve your overall quality of life.

To start this challenge, you must drop all the excuses for not cleaning your head and start now. When you start to tidy up, set a goal for yourself like "I want to clean the kitchen today" to help you stay focused and motivated during the process. Then, creating a regular schedule can also help you stay on top of the messes and avoid feeling overwhelmed.

To make it a fun and enjoyable activity, you can take a break by taking a short walk outside with your pet or relaxing by drinking a cup of coffee. You can also listen to your favorite music playlist and dance around as you clean. To keep your place tidy, you should always remind yourself to keep things organized and put them where they belong after use. You might not get used to this habit at first, but you should always adapt to being uncomfortable. Getting uncomfortable takes you places, which will be the focus of the next challenge.

### Challenge 3—Tidy Your Place

This challenge should not only be done this week, but you should make it a habit. For this week, the challenge is that you need to tidy up your things every day. By the end of the week, you should have at least a tidy room—or even a tidy house! For another extra challenge, you must drop "I will do it on the weekend or later" and just do it once and once only. After you succeed in this challenge, feel the change in your feelings while entering your already tidy place and your productivity level.

# Chapter 4:

# Get Uncomfortable

When was the last time you purposefully did something uncomfortable? Indeed, it is the only natural thing for people to seek a comfort zone in life, but it won't take you anywhere further. Anyone can get stuck in this so-called comfort zone, but you will get bored easily and crave a better "zone" the longer you stay there. Besides, remaining in your comfort zone will only lead to self-absorption, boredom, and a sense of discontent. If it happens to you right now, it is time for you to start challenging yourself in order to grow.

Growth always means stepping out of your comfort zone and doing something that you do not usually do. This is how we explore new territory outside of our comfort zone. We must get uncomfortable and get used to it. Often in life, we must perform in an uncomfortable situation or environment that brings new opportunities and experiences, whether it means giving a presentation to people that we do not know or talking to someone senior in our industry. Imagine you can get used to being uncomfortable; it prevents you from feeling overwhelmed or choking up.

To get out of your comfort zone, you need to make a habit of stepping outside of your usual self and doing an activity that prior to now seemed uncomfortable, scary, or needed a lot of effort to be done. A good way to get out of your comfort zone is to take small steps, such as initiating conversation with strangers, giving an important presentation at work, or even going to a party that used to make you afraid.

Getting uncomfortable by breaking a habit, trying something new, taking a risk, or throwing yourself into a totally new situation won't be easy, but I can guarantee that you will find it worthy and rewarding later. Embrace the growth through discomfort and see where it takes you!

To embrace being uncomfortable, you need to start recognizing how you feel when you face uncomfortable things. Later, this allows you to identify the types of experiences to seek out instead of turning away from them. Even just doing these uncomfortable things will help you develop skills around them. In order to be uncomfortable, you need to be open-minded and flexible to expose yourself to new experiences. Then, explore new experiences, even if they are different from what you are used to doing. Not limited to your uncomfortable things to do, you should expose yourself to and get comfortable with a totally new social setting.

Rather than being awkward, you should try to be more social while accepting the discomfort that comes with it. You will become a better conversationalist over time by learning to initiate interaction with people in various settings in order to make new friends. As mentioned earlier in this paragraph, it is important to first acknowledge yourself and your reality before challenging yourself further. Thus, the art of acknowledging yourself will be discussed in the next challenge.

### Challenge 4—Get Uncomfortable

This challenge is your initial sign to be ready to get uncomfortable as this book progresses. To do this challenge, you need to get uncomfortable and get used to it. If you find yourself to be an antisocial person, you need to greet people when you see them. If you are a social person, then you need to talk less to people. For the extra challenge, you should successfully overcome one of your uncomfortable actions.

# Chapter 5:

# Acknowledge Your Reality

We all have dreams, and we all have our ideal lifestyles. But where are we right now? Assessing and acknowledging where you are right now does not mean we are discouraged about how far we are from it, but rather that we are aware of how far we are and how we should begin to move forward step by step. Have you ever noticed how easy it is to give other people advice but how difficult it is to give yourself advice? By acknowledging your reality, you can see yourself in a bigger picture and then begin to embrace and accept it.

Do not confuse acceptance with resignation! Sometimes, most people assume that acceptance means lowering the bar, stopping caring, or just giving up on your dreams. In contrast, we can't even begin to improve something in our lives if we do not fully acknowledge and accept it at first. Recognizing and accepting your reality requires you to stop trying to change what you can and instead focus on what you can control—yourself. Acceptance is not giving up on your dreams, but rather ceasing to fight a futile battle with life.

Acceptance allows you to reduce feelings of shame, guilt, and anxiety if you haven't succeeded in achieving your dreams. The act of acceptance can reduce distress when dealing with negative thoughts and events that have happened in your life. Further, acceptance of coping skills is linked to lower rates of mental illness and suicide (Li and Zhang, 2012). To start accepting your reality, you should first notice when you are fighting against it. Realizing that you are refusing your reality is a great start toward accepting it.

If you feel bitter, and resentful and think that life is unfair to you, then you are probably fighting your reality. Keep in mind, you cannot undo the past! You must find peace within reality by determining what you can and cannot control. In embracing these feelings of failure, I want you to feel that it is okay to be angry, scared, overwhelmed, or even sometimes lonely. Physically relaxing your body can help you feel more ready to accept reality through meditation, taking a hot bath, getting a massage, or doing deep breathing exercises.

If you believe in positive affirmation, you can always use coping statements by repeating them to get through difficult times, such as "It is what it is" or "I can't change the past, but I can accept it and move forward". Accepting your reality and how you cannot control it is surely painful at first, but all you need is to mindfully practice it. If you don't master it immediately, you shouldn't be discouraged but rather give it another try until you get used to it.

You can always start accepting your reality, which often appears as an obstacle in your everyday life, even in smaller situations such as when you are stuck in traffic, when your internet is slow, or when your package takes too long to arrive. By practicing acceptance daily, it will be easier to use it as a coping tool when there are bigger and tougher challenges in the future. After accepting your reality, you can fully understand yourself and will be ready to set your dream goal for the future. Setting a goal is important for you to ensure that you run straight to the finish line, so it will be the focus of the next challenge.

### Challenge 5—Acknowledge Your Reality

To start this challenge, you should assess your life situation and fully understand where you are at. Keep in mind that it is okay to feel resentful at first, especially if you feel like going anywhere near your goal! For the extra challenge, you can envision where you want to be, as it will be easier after accepting your reality.

# Chapter 6:

# Set Your Goal

Are you one of the many people who make the same New Year's resolutions every year? Do you vow to yourself once more that you will complete the same task? If you choose yes, you are not alone. Many people are caught in a vicious loop where they create a goal, lose track of it, and end up not accomplishing it, then set the same goal again with a new desire to accomplish it. But the cycle can be broken.

Get the most out of your work and yourself by learning more about the goal-setting process. Keep in mind that it's like sailing without a destination in the ocean if we don't have a goal. Goals are like islands: once you board one, you go on to the next one. It's as if you replenish your stock each time you reach your objective (land on the island). And you can go again.

When you set goals, you create a long-term vision and short-term motivation. It focuses on your acquisition of knowledge and helps you manage your time and resources. It's all about making the most of your life. Setting precise and well-defined goals allows you to track your progress and make progress in what might have previously looked like a never-ending grind. As you become more aware of your own talent and skill in achieving the goals you've established, your self-confidence will also increase.

If goals are so important, why do we fail to achieve them? It is mainly because we don't plan the steps to get there. Before setting your goal, take a closer look at what you're trying to achieve and ask yourself whether this objective is something you want and whether it is essential enough to devote time and effort to.

SMART criteria, which stands for specific, measurable, achievable, realistic, and time-bound, is a particular way to set your goals. The key to making SMART goals is to be specific so that you can track your progress and determine whether you met those objectives. The more specific you can be with your goal, the higher the chance you'll complete it.

Setting goals for your life is pointless if you don't have a strategy or an action plan for how you'll achieve them. Your action plan should consist of the overall goal you're trying to achieve and all the steps you need to take to get there.

As part of your action plan, a timeline allows you to visualize roles, milestones, and deadlines to achieve your goal. A timeline creates a sense of urgency to motivate you to stay on schedule. Once you've set your goals, most people often distract themselves from directly achieving them. That's why you need to stay away from entertainment to avoid getting distracted by it, which will be the focus of the next challenge.

### Challenge 6—Set Your Goal

For this week, you need to challenge yourself by setting your goals in the form of a 1-year goal, 3-year goal, or 5-year goal. Don't be in a rush when deciding and setting your goal! Just focus on yourself and the things you truly have a passion to do. For the extra challenge, you can step-by-step identify what you need to achieve your goals in terms of certain experiences, classes, or other resources.

# Chapter 7:

# No Entertainment

How much time do we usually spend on entertainment each day? Is it three hours per day? Or more than five hours per day? You might not realize how many hours you waste seeking entertainment daily. Most people use 55% of their waking hours or roughly 8-9 hours per day attending entertainment media (Rentfrow et al, 2011). Entertainment media that people most use are music, television series or movies, games, and social media. Today, we are in an information overload era where hundreds of media, technologies, and notifications are competing for your attention.

In the last few years, it is no wonder that our attention spans have become shorter and shorter as our focus has also decreased. Stop undervaluing your already limited time in the world! Not being able to focus has numerous negative effects on how successful we are at work and in our personal lives.

Don't you want to live your life to the fullest? Most people don't put much thought into their own improvement and growth. They don't make time for learning and creativity, instead drowning themselves in the pursuit of endless entertainment. They tend to always seek entertainment and distraction, not learning and improving. As a result, they are stuck with the job they hate. They live their lives full of disappointment without knowing what to do. Do you still want your life to be in mediocrity?

If you want to start a no-entertainment habit, the key is to pick one task and eliminate the rest, realizing that nothing that is not required to complete the task is a distraction. If you haven't noticed the distractions that are keeping you from finishing your work, you need to identify the things or media that cause them. Then, you need to look for ways to set boundaries in the future to avoid those distractions from happening again.

Some people find their phone to be the biggest distraction, as they can't be without it for even a few minutes. Constant notifications from apps and text can distract you, let alone millions of contents uploaded every day in the form of videos or photos. Thus, setting boundaries for the use of your phone is the best way to stop distractions.

A simple way to significantly reduce distractions is to disable push notifications for as many apps as possible. Then, avoid making your phone the last thing you see before bed and the first thing you see when you wake up. If you use a conventional alarm clock and charge your phone somewhere out of sight, you won't be tempted to check it first thing in the morning and eventually during the day.

If you want to monitor your progress in the no-entertainment habit, you can review your daily or weekly entertainment media usage so you can see how well you stick to it. Once you've reduced your distraction, and put away entertainment, you now have spare time to do self-care, which allows you to have a healthier lifestyle. Thus, self-care will be the focus of the next challenge.

### *Challenge 7—No Entertainment*

To start this challenge, you need to drop all your inner desire to seek entertainment and focus more on doing and achieving goals. For this week, you cannot have entertainment, which means no games, TV, movies, or whatever it is! Once you've successfully done it, for an extra challenge, you can go for a walk each day and have a quiet week instead.

# Chapter 8:

# Self-Care

How often do you feel bad and sick inside after not taking care of yourself by consuming unhealthy food? Is it after eating junk food and highly processed food, chugging alcohol, or smoking a pack of cigarettes per day? Why won't you simply take care of your body as the only place you have to live? Most of us must have heard about the importance of self-care or what we "should" do for self-care. Not limited to taking yourself to the gym, meditating, or getting check-ups, the most important form of self-care is good nutrition, as it creates a better sense of balance in your life.

So why is it that self-care is still so hard to do? It is because many of us tend to prioritize our day-to-day duties in the following order: wake up, work or school, get tired, and sleep. We consistently put a self-care routine as our last thing to do, which can be easily skipped entirely if we run out of time or are tired. If you want to change this, changing your eating habits should be the most important act of self-care. You need to realize that frequent junk food eating contributes to a higher risk of obesity, diabetes, strokes, cancer, heart attacks, and even dementia. Aside from your physical health, there is a strong link between poor eating habits and mental illness and a decline in intelligence (Fuhrman, 2018).

The best way to make healthy eating a habit is to make it as simple, achievable, and realistic as possible. Start small and let's start focusing on self-caring ourselves to avoid consuming unhealthy lifestyles! To cut junk food and highly processed food, you can swap them for less processed food and fresh products. Cutting out junk food does not mean you can't enjoy your meal because healthier food can be as tasty or even tastier than junk food.

For inspiration, you can swap cookies for real fruit, a bag of chips for homemade unbuttered popcorn, milkshakes for homemade smoothies, or skip the processed meat on your pizza topping. By switching to a healthier choice, you can regain your taste buds' sensitivity after eating junk food that dulls them. Later, you'll find yourself preferring or even craving whole foods rather than junk food. Those of you who want to limit your alcohol intake can try to limit the amount of alcohol in the house or avoid it entirely. If you have no alcohol, you won't be tempted to drink it! As an alternative, you can stock any healthier beverage, including variants of tea, low-sugar soda, yogurt drinks, and fruit-infused water.

Quitting smoking is not an easy thing to do, but it's not impossible. Your body will thank you for your effort! To start limiting your smoking habit, you need to avoid the triggers where you occasionally smoked most often like going to bars or parties. You can also chew on sugarless gum, hard candy, or crunchy foods like raw carrots or nuts to resist a tobacco craving. Besides that, you can exercise away from the urge to smoke such as squats, running up and down stairs, or pushups.

From the tips mentioned before, you can practice self-care by simply shopping for what you need, which is healthy for you. The habit of shopping only for what you need may seem simple, but it's so much harder than that. Thus, it will be the focus of the next challenge.

### Challenge 8—Self-Care

For this week, you need to stay away from fast food, deep-fried food, and any other unhealthy habits, including smoking or drinking alcohol. After a week, you will feel so much better about your physical and mental health. For an added challenge, you can be creative in your meal preparation by learning healthy recipes and cooking every meal yourself.

# Chapter 9:

# Shop Only What You Need

How often have you found yourself shopping because something looked cool and cute, or simply because it was on sale? Then, only later, you realized that you didn't really need it. Many times, you probably ended up regretting your purchase and only wore it once. If not shopping, how often do you take yourself to a fancy dinner or buy luxury goods with a disguise of "self-reward" while later feeling bad about it?

I am not saying that you can't do self-reward at all, but why do you want to self-reward yourself if you're only going to regret it later? You should realize that you don't need all those luxury and fancy goods. All those luxury options are satisfying. It is not about being hard on yourself or about the money; it is about the mindset. Trying to keep up with luxury options will only add to your workload!

You need to stick to fulfilling the only three basic needs of humans: food, clothing, and shelter. Those three needs are the ones you need, not the ones you want. Live on the bare minimum, with no luxury options! Besides, you need to learn to shop consciously and sustainably. When you want to buy anything, you need to ask yourself first whether you need this item. The goal is to be intentional with all your purchases to avoid them being useless and wasted.

Before setting foot in any store, you need to have a shopping list and stick to it, no matter what. This tip will effectively help you resist the urge to make a spontaneous purchase. Once you get to the store, there is no need to wander around; stick to the shopping list, go to the relevant section, make your purchases, and leave. Not only are you saving money, but you are also saving a lot of time. A budget plan is an essential tool to map out your expenses and keep your spending on track. Once you've made a budget plan, completely rule out a credit card to purchase things.

When you've successfully adopted these spending habits, the most important thing is to resist the pressure to have the same luxury and fancy things as your peers or, worse, celebrities. Stop trying to keep up with the Kardashians! On this challenge, you may realize that being close to things you love can potentially be the hardest addiction to kick—in this case, luxurious options. Staying away from what you love allows you to achieve more and squeeze in more time to work on yourself, which will be the focus of the next challenge.

## Challenge 9—Shop Only What You Need

For this week, you need to only buy what you need and stick with your shopping list. Planning it out a few days before getting to the store will help you sort out the most needed ones. For the extra challenge, you can't do any shopping other than for your basic needs or stacking your goods.

# Chapter 10:

# Stay Away from What You Love

Being able to do what we love is a blessing. But do you remember that when you were young, you could only play games over the weekends, even if you absolutely loved them and wanted to play them every single day? It means that staying away from it has meaning. In real life, we must make sacrifices and give up certain things from time to time. Adopting the mindset that we can stay away from what we love when it matters the most.

Whether you change your lifestyle just so you can achieve more or squeeze in more time to work on yourself. This is since a feeling of love for an object can seriously lead to addiction, such as to certain music, games, types of food, types of drinks, or even specific activities. People in love with an object often experience some behaviors associated with addiction, including euphoria, craving, or even dependency (Hill, 2019).

Addiction is a complicated disease that not only affects the physical body but also crushes mental health. Excessive love for an object can lead to taking a toll on a relationship, irresponsible behaviors, family commitments, and work duties. Thus, staying away from what you love is essential for you to achieve more and work on yourself.

Excessive love or addiction to certain things can be caused by the need to escape from boring routines at school, work, or home. Alternatively, you can start by thoughtfully self-exploring. Have you found exactly what you want from life? If you haven't, this is the right time for you to do some self-discovery. In self-discovery, you may end up finding your true self, personal values, personality traits, hidden talent, or even long-lost dreams. These things may not always seem to matter much in the chaos of daily life, but awareness of these characteristics can give you insight into your inner and truest self.

Self-discovery sounds like an intimidating process at first, but it just really means that you need to examine your life while figuring out what's missing and taking steps to fulfill it. During this process, you can explore your passions to give your life purpose and make it more meaningful.

Living out your passion may help you identify the job you want and find the steps necessary for your future career. Then, you can increase and use your passion to boost your confidence and encourage you to keep exploring other talents that you might not have noticed before. Staying away from what you love will make you realize that it is important to appreciate what you have right now. Thus, it will be the focus of the next challenge to not take things in life for granted.

### Challenge 10—Stay Away from What You Love

For this challenge, you might need to push yourself harder than before by staying away from an object or an activity you love the most. In this challenge, I strictly do not challenge you to stay away from people you love. Before initiating this challenge, you can list as many things as possible or objects you love and decide to stay away from the first one of them. For the extra challenge, you must stay away from the three top ones from that list.

# Chapter 11:

# Appreciate What You Have

You may already have heard everyone so often say, "Don't take things for granted." We all often take certain things for granted, some more than others. It's time to ask yourself. Do you ever do it in your life? Do you really understand what it means? Not taking things for granted does not simply mean being grateful for what you have; it's also about changing your mindset and your belief that everything in your life will always be available or stay the same. Just because you are getting used to what you have right now, you must be aware that nothing really stays forever, whether it is the ability to do or buy something or the people staying around you. Often in life, nothing can be guaranteed for tomorrow. Thus, we must treasure them while they are still here.

Not taking things for granted is not only to be grateful but also to understand how blessed you are and use that positive energy as fuel for something greater. We are all far more fortunate than we realize because we frequently focus on the things and situations we lack. Appreciation and gratitude for what you have unlocked a sense of the content of life and turn what we have into enough or even more than enough. Gratitude brings a feeling of peace for today and creates a better vision for the future.

To start being appreciative and grateful for what you have, you need to slow down occasionally, to ensure that you realize every little thing to be grateful for. Being in the chaos and rush of life can eventually make you forget to appreciate your life itself. Then, you can use this appreciation on the outside by expressing gratitude to others.

In the easiest way, you can grasp every opportunity to say thank you to others, no matter how small the instance. Gratitude journaling can be a way to practice gratitude, as it is easy to take things for granted, especially if we're not even aware of them in the first place. When you're feeling sad, practicing gratitude keeps you from shifting to a more rounded and positive view.

If you feel like you're taking all the things you have for granted, you can try to be less materialistic and more frugal. If you learn to be more frugal, you'll realize that all the things you have are luxuries rather than ordinary things to have, especially if you compare yourself to less fortunate people around you.

Other than the media around you, your phone can be one of the most influential media, making you often compare your possessions to celebrities' luxuries which makes you take things for granted. So, reducing and staying away from your phone may help you appreciate what you have in real life. Thus, keeping away from phones will be the focus of the next challenge.

### *Challenge 11—Appreciate What You Have*

This week's challenge may seem simple, but it allows you to really see what you need to be grateful for. In this challenge, you need to write down what you are grateful for each day. For the extra challenge, you must show appreciation to people who provide you with something, even in a small and seemingly simple instance.

# Chapter 12:

# No Phones

Have you ever checked your phone's screen time? You probably don't think that you use it that much, but how often have you realized that you are on the phone more when you are hanging out with your friends? Are you suffering from nomophobia? Maybe you are still unfamiliar with the term "nomophobia," but I am sure that you know someone who is suffering from it, or maybe it's yourself. Nomophobia refers to the worry or fear that individuals experience when they are unable to use their phones. It was found that two out of every three people suffered from nomophobia (SecurEnvoy, 2012).

So, how can you tell if you tend to overuse your phone? There are some potential indicators, such as you often feeling anxious or upset when you aren't on your phone; you immediately reaching for your phone when you're slightly bored or alone; you're spending more and more time on your phone; and your phone use interferes with your work or school performance, which also affects your relationship with others in real life. Several personality traits have been associated with unhealthy, overused, and problematic phone use, including low self-esteem, anxiety, depression, being highly extroverted, and sleep disturbance (De-Sola Gutiérrez, 2016).

If you already feel that your phone use is affecting your health, mental health, work/school performance, or relationship, it's time to change your habits. First, you need to change some settings on your phone to reduce the tendency to frequently check your phone. You should change your settings to eliminate push notifications, as those little "ding" sounds can trigger you to immediately check them.

If your work is closely related to checking emails or social media, you can decide in advance the specific time when you can check those work-related apps on the phone. Then, you need to keep your phone out of sight, especially when you are in bed, to ensure that the phone is not the last and first thing you look at during the day.

When you put your phone out of reach, it's easier to avoid checking it for no reason. To entirely replace the habit of phone overuse, you need to pick up a new hobby or develop new skills through real-world activities like meeting up with new friends, painting, doing volunteer work, cooking, gardening, or even yoga and meditation. These tips may seem simple, but once you slack off, you'll end up with the same phone overuse again and again. Don't catch yourself slacking! Thus, it will be further discussed in the next challenge.

## *Challenge 12—No Phones*

For this week's challenge, you cannot use your phone, except for necessary work purposes and real-life emergencies. I understand it may be an urgent matter, so I only encourage this challenge to be done outside of work purposes. If you're expecting an important phone call or notification this week, you can swap this challenge with another and come back to it later. For the extra challenge, you should resist the urge to check it too frequently, whenever you want to.

# Chapter 13:

# No Slacking

How often do you feel discouraged and powerless when the deadline is near? Do you realize that you often slack off, affecting your work or school performance? Some signs that show you're slacking off are underestimating your task, finding it delightful to extend deadlines, scrolling your phone between tasks, or decreasing overall performance. If you've often done these activities without even realizing it, it has already become your mentality. Being discouraged is a normal thing, but do not let it decrease your performance in the long term and define who you are.

Slacking off can be due to many factors, including tiredness from doing a task repeatedly, dislike of your task in the first place, or an unclear idea of task responsibilities. These conditions cause you to slack, which raises your stress level, causes you to miss targets frequently, and causes you to pass up opportunities. Once you've noticed that you frequently slack off, you need to set the tone and keep it that way for the rest of the week, which can later be adapted to new habits. This is the right way to build us to be the best version of ourselves—a role model, a symbol, or whatever you want to call it. You need to put it all out there and push further.

First, you should avoid multitasking, as it most likely decreases your productivity greatly if you are constantly switching from one task to another. Thus, it will significantly increase your stress level during the task. So, when you focus on one thing at a time, you must assess the priorities of tasks and prioritize them. To avoid slacking off, you can break your big project into smaller chunks and then assign a deadline to every chunk that you create.

During tasks, you should take a break now and then to make sure your mind is more focused, and you can work more effectively. Then, limit yourself to distractions around you to prevent you from getting sidetracked, so you need to refrain from using your phone and avoid using social media, as already mentioned in the previous challenge. Avoiding the urge to slack off does not mean that you need to sacrifice your sleep time; you need to schedule your sleep instead. Having a scheduled sleep time helps you be more focused during the day, which will be further discussed in the next challenge.

### Challenge 13—No Slacking

For this week's challenge, you need to do whatever you do at your best and optimal state. Don't ever catch yourself slacking off! Push yourself to the limit! For the extra challenge, you need to put all your efforts in and further explore how you can even do it better than you previously were.

# Chapter 14:

# Schedule Your Sleep

How many hours did you sleep today? Do you feel energized from your sleep? If you're regularly waking up needing some more hours of sleep, then it is time to reschedule your bedtime. Sleep is an essential function of the human body that allows the mind and body to recharge, resulting in a refreshed and alert state in the morning. Without enough sleep, the brain cannot function properly, which leads to impaired abilities and performance. Moreover, inadequate sleep leads to various health issues such as hypertension, obesity, impaired immune functioning, cardiovascular disease, mood disorders, and even loneliness (Worley, 2018).

If you want to improve your overall health, get better-quality sleep and not only focus on the duration of your sleep. The first and most essential thing to understand, you need to identify the causes of your inadequate or interrupted sleep. Is it your work shift that demands you work at night? Is it because of the blue lights from digital screens you watched at night? Do you have fluctuating sleep hours that prevent you from having a steady sleep pattern? Did you drink caffeine and energy drinks at night? Know yourself to improve yourself!

Once you've found the cause of your inadequate sleep, you should gradually eliminate it from your sleeping habits. To adjust your bedtime, you need to be patient while slowly increasing in small increments of time until you are at the desired hour you want to sleep. Then, do not nap even if you feel tired, as napping can delay your sleepiness at night.

In scheduling your sleep, you must be consistent to maintain a functioning sleep schedule and not snooze your alarm in the morning, even on the weekends. Optimizing your bedroom atmosphere is an effective way to improve sleep quality. You can do this by keeping dim lights around your bed, making the temperature cool, turning off all electronics, and adding a relaxing scent.

Before sleeping, you can take a warm bath or play some relaxing music to help you wind down. In scheduling your sleep, it is important that you already measure your time well. Between school, work, hobbies, or other important activities, it is recommended to get 7–8 hours of sleep to be well-rested the next day. Measuring your time in a day is needed to ensure you already use your time effectively; thus, it will be the focus of the next challenge.

### *Challenge 14—Schedule Your Sleep*

For this week's challenge, you need to schedule your sleeping time between 7–8 hours and try your best to stick to it until the end of the week. You can gradually adjust it until your desired bedtime. For the extra challenge, you should get to bed 10 minutes earlier than usual.

# Chapter 15:

# Measure Your Time

Everyone on this earth has the exact same 24 hours in a day, including Bill Gates, Mark Zuckerberg, Steve Jobs, Barack Obama, Oprah Winfrey, and us. So why do they manage to achieve more, yet we have the same amount of time? How can we use our time to do the most? It is all about efficiency and productivity. At one point or another, we have all struggled to manage our time better and more efficiently. So, if you are currently feeling all over the place, remember that time management can be learned if you are persistent and practice until it becomes an effortless habit. You need to stop wishing you had more hours in a day and begin to make them instead.

Time management is an important skill to help you organize your daily tasks, complete work on time, and prioritize your tasks. Whether you want to launch a new business, get promoted at work, finish your thesis on time, or even become healthier and happier, time management allows you to arrange a step-by-step approach from the moment you wake up until the moment you go to bed.

To start this challenge, you can make a to-do list to ensure you are productive. This to-do list should be made at the end of each day and consist of the tasks you need to accomplish for the following day. So, when you wake up, you can stick to the list without wondering what you're going to do that day. Not only push you to be productive, finishing and checking off your to-do list help you to motivate yourself to accomplish bigger projects and reduce the stress of being "not productive."

Besides the tasks that you need to do, the to-do list should consist of what you are supposed to do. It allows you to track how many times you need to complete a task and ensure that you are not doing it mindlessly. You can always use a timer app to help you review the time. From the result of tracking time, perhaps you can squeeze some time and use that extra time to achieve more. If you still feel like you need more time and want to achieve more, waking up earlier can be your immediate solution.

By getting up early, you will have enough time to better plan and prepare for your day. When you wake up late, you are most likely to spend the rest of the day unprepared and try to catch up with a sense of being behind. Is that not enough? Then, it's time for you to take advantage of your Sunday night rather than just having a lazy day.

On a Sunday night, you can prepare all the things you need for the following week, including organizing a priority list, arranging a to-do list, prepping meals, planning outfits for work, or even meditating to relax. The more you prepare yourself on Sunday night, the more time you can get to do things you need to work on the following week. By the end of the week, you can already see what you can improve in your daily life. Then, you can squeeze some time to do new things to be able to see yourself from a different angle, which will be the focus of the next challenge.

### *Challenge 15—Measure Your Time*

To start this challenge, you need to record your daily activities and the time spent on each of them. By the end of each day, you will get a factual report on the tasks you accomplished, and the exact time spent. This result helps you to analyze how you can use your time more effectively as an extra challenge. Every day is a new chance to become the better version of yourself that you always wanted to be, so make the most of your 24 hours.

## Chapter 16:

# A Different Angle

When was the last time you did something new for the first time? If you haven't done it yet, what are your excuses? Perhaps time is one of the most mentioned excuses for not discovering something new, whereas you already get overwhelmed by your daily chores and responsibilities. If we only stick to what we used to do, there won't be any changes, so we must do something that we are not used to doing and break the cycle. Breaking those barriers and aiming higher can open doors of opportunity for you.

Previously, we already learned time management so from that spare time we should utilize it to embark on new adventures. Besides, we frequently let our own fears stop us from discovering new angles in our lives. Whereas, once we've done something new, it keeps our lives exciting. So, what are you waiting for? Seizing every opportunity or spare time you have is one of the most important actions to be taken. To start this challenge, you can try a small activity, skill, or something that is the most possible for you. If you start with a rather small and spontaneous activity, it can give you less pressure, and then you can build yourself up to bigger things.

There are endless choices that you can try to make. Don't ever try to put yourself in a box! Traveling is one of the most gratifying ways to explore your world in another country, another city, or even another side of your city. It allows you to discover and learn new things based on its culture, landscape, and architecture. If you have no spare time to travel, you can always try a new activity on your bucket list. Don't worry about the result and keep an open mind! Whatever the result, at least you gave it a shot and just moved on to other adventures that may suit your fancy.

Besides, you can attend a different event from your usual liking to get outside of your comforts such as a music concert, festival, exhibition, sport or competition show, and fashion show. Later, you will be surprised at what you end up enjoying. If you are adventurous in the kitchen, you can try out a new restaurant that specializes in a cuisine you rarely eat. Later, you can grocery shop for new ingredients and make your own dish. These activities will make your life content and fulfilling while you explore new adventures.

While trying new things, you might face lots of challenges and obstacles, but never take that personally. Taking it too personally makes you hesitant to try another new thing; just see the challenge as a new experience. Thus, the art of not taking anything personally is the focus of next week's challenge.

### Challenge 16—A Different Angle

For this week's challenge, you should start to reflect on your time usage from last week and free up 30 minutes a day. Then, try something during those 30 minutes. For the extra challenge, you can free up an hour and try another new activity. Be fearless or you may regret it in the future!

# Chapter 17:

# Not Personal

Everyone makes mistakes all the time, whether you are a parent, celebrity, lecturer, businessman, or even the president. So, if things don't live up to your expectations, don't blindly blame yourself; rather, consider your mistake as a part of learning. When was the last time you blamed yourself? How did you feel after that? Taking your mistake personally will not help you solve the problem; rather, it will draw you away from the solution. Dwelling on your mistake will only intensify the negative feelings toward yourself.

Think about how many fights we have had in our lives. Looking back on them, does it really matter now? We must understand that emotion is temporary, and we must learn how to control our emotions, even at the toughest times. So that we can see the truth or the whole picture clearly, as emotion will cloud our thoughts. It may be tough, but to get where you want to be, you must start forgiving yourself.

Not taking it personally does not mean that we need to blame others for the problems we have. How often do we blame someone when things don't go as planned? Typically, we choose to blame others as an easy way to avoid the feeling of guilt. If you've often done it, you will find yourself not realizing that you have any flaws and don't need to change for the better.

To start this challenge, you need to view your mistakes in life as an opportunity for self-improvement rather than viewing them as failures. However, you must accept responsibility for your error and resolve to become a better version of yourself. You should take responsibility for your behavior and view the encounter as a learning opportunity. You do not have to face the end of the world as a result of a mistake you made. Keep moving forward with the knowledge and experience you gained through your toughest moments.

When facing problems in life, we all must have felt discouraged and taken a couple of steps back. Do you ever have days like that? If you feel these emotions, it is time for you to identify the source, admit it, and then move forward to seek a solution. You must remember that every problem has a solution, and it's just a matter of time until you find it. When you recover from negative emotions, you feel better and have more clarity, which allows you to find solutions more quickly.

Instead of dwelling on your mistakes, it's critical to focus on solutions and act. Previously, I've been told not to blame others, as they must have their own weaknesses just like you and everybody else in the world. Even if you know their weaknesses, you still need to be respectful of them. Thus, being respectful of others is as important as being respectful of yourself, so this will be the focus of the next challenge.

## Challenge 17—Not Personal

To start this challenge, you need to learn not to take it personally when shit happens, which will eventually happen throughout everybody's life. Keep in mind that you're not the only one suffering when dealing with a problem, and don't let it stop you from growing. For the extra challenge, you should focus on the solution and put your emotions to one side.

# Chapter 18:

# Be Respectful

Do you realize how diverse we are in this world? There are numerous differences in people's culture, race, religion, and even abilities. This diversity is often seen as a difficulty for many people, whereas this diversity allows people to learn different skills, talents, and experiences. So, we must understand everyone comes from different backgrounds, just as we were raised with different kinds of support and opportunities with respect to others' appearance or social, economic, or personal background.

Being respectful to one another is the most essential element needed to create a positive environment in which relationships can flourish. even if we do not share the same values. So, we need to compromise with it by looking past other people's mistakes and disregarding our clashing beliefs with them. In other words, being respectful means selecting to see the good in people and appreciating their talents, skills, and what they can contribute to creating an inclusive environment to live in. Being respectful builds trust in one another, promotes good behavior, and makes you accept the rights of others to be themselves.

To fully appreciate an individual as he or she is, you need to show empathy and be considerate, even for their mistakes. These appreciations need to be evident in your actions to show your respect. To be close to anyone, you need to practice your active listening skills to show you are present and paying attention. Furthermore, active listening shows the other person that you really value the conversation. Throughout the conversation, you will find common ground in the form of shared experience or value. It will be simple to establish a positive relationship with them once you have found common ground.

When you are in a conflict, you can use the situation as a learning opportunity to gain their perspective instead of dwelling on the differences you have. You might or might not relate to their perspective, but you can respect their right to have it. Honoring one's perspective on certain things means honoring their overall background. Then, appreciating and affirming their perspective will give them a sense that they matter and are worthy of respect. By doing so, you will build positive feelings for one another and create a supportive and inclusive environment that benefits everyone.

While respecting others, you will find that each person has their own weaknesses and strengths, including yourself. Trying to understand others means trying to understand yourself in the bigger picture. Even if you later discover that you are superior to others, you must remain humble and create a safe space for criticism and improvement rather than blocking out all the noise and stagnation in your life. Thus, staying humble makes you better than just good, which will be the focus of the next challenge.

### Challenge 18—Be Respectful

Even if you already respect others, this challenge makes you more respectful to everyone by demonstrating your respect through actions. For the extra challenge, you need to look at everyone in the exact same way to treat them equally and respectfully.

# Chapter 19:

# Stay Humble

Why do we need to be humble? Many people might say that being humble is a weakness as it relates to having low opinions of yourself, low self-esteem, and not being confident. Meanwhile, it's the opposite, because being humble means understanding our values and acknowledging that we are good at certain things. Understanding our actual values and acknowledging our abilities can facilitate our efforts to improve ourselves. That realization also prevents you from believing that there is nothing else you can learn and from being overconfident.

Being humble makes us understand that there is always room for improvement. Only when we are humble will we see the opening and be able to break through. Being able to absorb different opinions and thoughts, rather than being overconfident and blocking all the noise. It is all in our mind; no matter how good we are, we can always be better. For our own well-being, becoming humble helps us navigate negative feelings better when we're dealing with losses. The humbler you are, the more resilient you can be in dealing with difficulties in life.

Being humble is a human quality that enables one's mind to be free of all resistance. A humble mind can listen to anything, praise or criticism, without getting aroused in rage at having their weaknesses exposed or being puffed up in self-righteousness at their own virtue. This quality is particularly helpful for learning lessons for life because there is no obstacle to their own progress. An intellectually humble person can pay more attention to a new lesson, have a better recognition memory, and absorb their lesson far more quickly than an arrogant one (Deffler et al., 2016).

The other characteristic of humble people is a better sense of forgiveness. Even if you verbally criticize them, their humility will counteract your attack because they have no resentment, which often results in a disagreement. Even in this challenge, you've learned to stay humble, but that does not mean that you must devalue yourself by saying sorry too often. Keep in mind to say sorry when necessary to not let people run over you so easily, which will be the focus of the next challenge.

## *Challenge 19—Stay Humble*

For this week's challenge, you need to find ways to improve your best skill by remaining humble. Staying humble ensures you crave more learning and never stop learning with other people. For the extra challenge, you must have an open mind and dare to try or explore new things from new people.

# Chapter 20:

# Stop Saying Sorry

"Sorry for complaining so much," "Sorry for being late," "Sorry to interrupt you," or "Sorry for letting you down." Does either of these phrases sound familiar to you? How often have you done it this week? If you've often done it, maybe you've been over apologizing this whole time, which has become a common reflex reaction for you.

Sorry means that we are feeling regret, sympathy, sorrow, and pity for the other person, but we don't often use it for these purposes. Instead, we keep saying sorry when asking a question, complaining, or even asking for help instead of apologizing. This overuse of apologizing can backfire on you. You might consider yourself a caring person by saying sorry all the time, but you're displaying that you have low self-esteem, self-doubt, and powerlessness toward your own actions.

When you constantly apologize, it can often feel exhausting and annoying for other people. Then, it will become less sincere and heartfelt when you need to say sorry for your mistakes. Later, this habit of saying sorry can compromise your professional values, as you often focus on others' perceptions of you.

To avoid the overuse of an apology, you need to understand its actual use and the appropriate situations in which to express it. An apology is only appropriate when you say or do something offensive, hurt someone's feelings, or offend their boundaries. Instead, you don't have to apologize for things you can't control, like asking for help, asking a question, or not having all the answers.

To start this challenge, you need to rethink why you apologized previously. If it's something that you shouldn't apologize for, you need to start noticing it and catch yourself in the act. Then, you'll become aware of when and why you mostly apologize.

Once you've identified certain situations in which you are saying sorry, you need to mindfully substitute the phrase "Sorry" to "Thank you", which turns apologetic phrases into ones that radiate confidence more. Instead of saying "Sorry for being late", you can say "Thank you for waiting" or "Thank you for your patience". When responding to a complaint, you can say, "Thank you for bringing this to my attention" or "Thank you for flagging this issue".

If there is a minor issue you need to address, you can focus on solutions rather than only apologizing for it by saying, "I hear you, and I am going to solve this issue soon", "This didn't go as planned, but I can assure you that I will fix it" or "Can you give me feedback on how I can do it better?" Instead of using "Sorry" to express sympathy, you can practice empathy by acknowledging others' feelings over your own.

Rather than saying "Sorry to hear that", you can say "That must have been really difficult for you" or "What can I do to make it easier for you?" Besides stopping saying sorry, it is important for you to hold a feeling of anger within yourself because it often clouds you to make a bad decision. Thus, managing your anger will be the focus of the next challenge.

### Challenge 20—Stop Saying Sorry

For this week's challenge, you need to stop saying "Sorry" when it is not necessary. You should swap sorry with other phrases or expressions which better exude confidence in you.

# Chapter 21:

# Chew in The Anger

When you are angry, do you know why you are angry? What is the real reason(s) behind it, whether physical, mental, or spiritual? We all experience anger every now and then when dealing with difficult situations. Sometimes, a wave of anger is a completely natural emotion that can be helpful in dealing with hard times, giving us a push to stand up for ourselves and potentially protecting us from immediate danger. Thus, you need to deal with anger in a positive way.

Do you ever feel your anger piling up inside of you and leaving you feeling out of control? Does your anger take a toll on your mental or physical health, and does your relationship with others interfere with your day-to-day life? Once you've identified these feelings in yourself, it's time for you to differentiate between healthy short-term anger and overwhelming rage.

Problematic anger is indicated when you become physically violent, feel unable to control it, threaten other people's safety, and feel impatient or hostile. Besides, the negative emotion of anger can potentially decrease our ability to reason because our brain is only focused on the emotional state rather than concentrating on making decisions. Most of the time, anger can cloud your mind and force you to make a bad decision. If you feel these risks of anger, remember that you have the power to change and overcome them.

If you are experiencing anger, there are some actions you can take to control your emotions. When anger strikes, it's easy to get swept up in the wave of emotion. To take control and reduce feelings of anger, you can instead focus on your breathing by taking slow, deep, controlled breaths. It can offer you some time to gather your thoughts, calm down, and react in a way that won't have an adverse long-term impact.

In the heat of the moment, it's easy to say something you'll later regret. Before you speak, you should take a moment to gather your thoughts while closing your eyes in a calm space and picturing yourself in a relaxing scene. Later, you'll feel restored to a more balanced emotional state.

During this time, you'll discover that spending time alone helps you manage your emotions more effectively because you're able to see the bigger picture and approach a situation from a different angle. This doesn't mean that you shouldn't show your anger at all, but it does mean that you need to do so in a controlled manner.

Instead of outbursts, having an intimate and mature conversation is more helpful to relieve stress, calm anger, and prevent future issues. Then, you can channel your anger into a tangible production such as painting, gardening, exercising, writing, or other activities you find relaxing.

Additionally, forgiving those who hurt you is a powerful tool to prevent uncontrollable anger, as now you are releasing weight. If you let anger and negative emotions overpower the positive ones, you are most likely to be dominated by your own bitterness or sense of injustice.

It's important to not let your anger lead you toward feeling sorrow. It is okay to not be okay for a certain period, but don't let that drag you down for too long. Thus, the art of bouncing back from hard times will be the focus of the next challenge.

### Challenge 21—Chew in The Anger

To start this challenge, you need to hold the anger within yourself and understand its triggers. Later, you'll find that you understand yourself a little more and a trauma that you probably have leading you to anger issues. For the extra challenge, you should dive deeper into your thoughts and be honest with yourself, with the goal of understanding yourself more than before.

# Chapter 22:

# Suck Up the Tears

"It's okay to not be okay" and "When life gives you lemons, make lemonade" are motivational phrases that you might often hear. Do you really know what this means? These phrases are used to inspire optimism even when you're in hard times and embrace life in whatever form. It does not imply that you can or are able to simply brush your problems off your shoulders.

Sometimes, it seems like one thing goes wrong after another, whether you hate your job, your anxiety is eating you up, you are still battling with bad habits, you often make your own mistakes, or you feel like you're not there yet. You should stop resisting feeling "bad", sometimes it's better for you to admit that you are lonely, lost, or unmotivated.

We all understand what it's like to "not be okay", so don't worry about what other people are doing. We all experience these emotions from time to time; thus, they are all normal and valid. Is it a fun place to be? Absolutely not, but it doesn't last forever, and your feelings are temporary. You can let those overwhelming emotions rule for a while by stopping the activities that keep you sane, joyful, and motivated.

Sometimes, we should all be allowed to fall apart so that we can discover ourselves all over again. It might be that your vision is a little fuzzy right now, but you need it to trust the process, trust yourself, and later pick yourself up. It is okay to not be okay for a certain period, but don't let that drag you down for too long and define who you are. It takes a lot of courage to bounce back from difficult situations, and it is surely not easy, but eventually we will.

Consider your life a roller coaster; you'll never know when to expect the ups and downs. One day you make everything happen in the blink of an eye, and the next you feel everything you've built crumbling.

When you're going through the ups and downs of life, remember to bounce back faster than ever before. If you can't find a way, you need to find a way to bounce back.

To successfully bounce back, you need to reframe the way you think about stressful moments in your life. Rather than thinking, "I'm a failure, I can't do this anymore", you can think that "This moment is temporary and is merely a setback; I'll get through this soon". If you are still struggling to manage your emotions, remembering how you navigated and conquered difficult times in the past can be helpful.

Once you've managed your emotions well, you need to look at the bright side of these previous hard times. Later, you'll feel more empowered and motivated to find a solution to the problem. You can see these times as an opportunity to learn new skills, knowledge, and moral values. The more you know about the ups and downs of life, the more adept you'll be at handling and better reacting to those situations.

When life knocks you down hard, you have two choices: get up and move forward or stay on the ground and mourn losses. The next time that life knocks you down, you need to bounce back fast without even self-doubt or second thoughts about it because it will be harder for you to get up again the longer you stay down.

Keep in mind that every struggle that happens is only a steppingstone closer to your goal. So, what are you waiting for? Just take a step, no matter how small or big, to give yourself a sense of accomplishment, and keep going. You are not the only person suffering in hard times, so don't focus on yourself as the victim of how unfair life is. When you have that kind of victim mentality, you'll be stuck wherever you are right now. Thus, how to stop this victim mentality will be the focus of the next challenge.

### Challenge 22—Suck Up the Tears

For this week's challenge, you need to stop crying inside when things go south; instead, you should focus on the solution and how to make things better. For the extra challenge, you should make yourself get used to bouncing back quickly after your downs in life.

# Chapter 23:

# Stop the Victim Mentality

It is impossible to avoid negative events in our lives, but we can control our reactions and thoughts about them. Are you one to bounce back or blame the world for what happened? When something bad occurs in life, indeed, it's easy to let your emotions ride the wave rather than reflect inside. However, if it gets out of hand, it's easy to start floundering in a victim mentality.

When you have a victim mentality, you tend to catastrophe problems by always expecting the worst from every problem, no matter how minor. You'll always think that "I'll never get this job", "I'll never get past this; it's impossible", or "I can't do anything right ever". Then, you'll feel powerless and helpless when these bad things really happen, while blaming others and circumstances for your own failure.

Having a victim mentality closely relates to always doubting yourself, which results in self-sabotaging your best efforts, leading to anxiety, depression, and behavioral issues (Kets de Vries, 2012). If you often feel like the world constantly and intentionally makes you miserable, you have fallen deep into a victim mentality.

In fact, life's not out to get you. Even when you happen to have good things in life for a moment, you will find yourself always discounting the positive and thinking that "I didn't deserve this, it was pure luck". In life, numerous things happen that are out of your control, so your job is to decide how you're going to react to those events and start seeing them as opportunities for growth.

If you want to change this victim mentality inside of you, you need to start healing the probable factors that caused it. You may develop this mentality due to negative life events including betrayed trust, intense emotional pain, past trauma, or being manipulated. Healing your past self can assist you in overcoming traumatic experiences and breaking free from a victim mindset.

You need to address your wounds and shift your perspective by focusing on things that you can change in the future. Finding things that you can control can greatly help you get your power back and have the confidence to transform bad things into something better. Then, you should stop blaming others and realize that you have more control than you thought before.

Practicing gratitude can be one of the ways to be grateful for all the lessons that life teaches you, even the difficult ones. It's impossible to feel like a victim when you're already feeling grateful for your life. A victim mentality is grounded in a feeling that everything is never enough. Then, it's time for you to let go of the "victim" label and become a "survivor" in your life.

Becoming a survivor means acknowledging the strength and power within to continue moving forward. To avoid falling into a victim mentality anymore, you need to remember that life is a journey consisting of experiences and moments. So, if something seemingly undesirable occurs, all you need to do is take a lesson from it and keep on moving forward. You are the driver of your own life! So, if you want to be better, start immediately, no more excuses. Excuses will only hinder you from your own success, which will be further discussed in the next challenge.

### Challenge 23—Stop the Victim Mentality

For this week's challenge, you must not accept yourself as a victim in your life. When you have a victim mentality, you will not be able to see the truth or root cause and learn from a difficult situation. So, instead of wallowing in self-pity, you should stay strong and learn from the extra challenge.

# Chapter 24:

# No More Excuses,

# No Matter What!

Get your plans done, no matter what, put your mind to it!

As much as we hate to admit it, each one of us has made excuses in every aspect of our lives. Some of us use it every now and then, while others always make excuses, whether to get out of things we don't like doing, avoid trying something new, or simply refuse to step outside of our comfort zone. Making excuses is the easiest way out of situations that seem unpleasant or that cause you fear or anxiety. So why do people like to make excuses so much? Sometimes, we frequently use excuses to avoid committing to something or simply because we like to procrastinate instead of doing something, even though we know it's beneficial for us.

While some excuses might appear harmless, each excuse you make takes you a step further away from reaching your full potential. Perhaps people tend to like making excuses for not having a good start whether your parents are divorced, you only come from a suburb, or you didn't enroll in a reputable school. People can be so incredibly creative when it comes to making excuses.

Whatever your most dependable excuse is, you need to remind yourself that where you start has nothing to do with where you are going. Oftentimes, we only keep making excuses without acknowledging the consequences, as the more we use them, the harder it will be for us to get things done. That is when you know that you've crossed the line, and it's time to stop with the excuses before it's too late to be regretful.

To stop making excuses, you also need to stop dwelling on the past failures that have affected you so much. Focusing on the past is only making you feel worse about yourself, leading to making excuses to justify your failures rather than focusing on making things better. Then, you should stop comparing yourself to others' achievements because everyone is unique, and your life is your own journey. Remember, you should only compare yourself with yourself to focus on being your best self. Moreover, you need to learn to own your mistakes in difficult times rather than blaming things that aren't within your control.

When you take responsibility for your own mistakes, you will be able to not repeat those mistakes again and feel empowered to take charge of your life. While it's important to learn from your mistakes, you also need to be honest with yourself about your weaknesses and embrace the imperfection within.

Once you accept your weaknesses and mistakes, you need to create goals by keeping them realistic and attainable. Then, start trying to achieve them and not giving up. Hence, starting is always the hardest part, but once we get rolling and gain some momentum, it will be so much easier. So, get yourself moving!

Remember to not let your excuses define who you are, and it's time for you to start believing in yourself. Believing in yourself will greatly help you push yourself harder to reach your goals. Thus, believing in yourself will be the focus of the next challenge.

### Challenge 24—No More Excuses

To start this challenge, you need to first consider making excuses as a common thing to do. Then, you need to remember how those excuses hindered you from pursuing greater opportunities in the past. So, for this week's challenge, you need to stop making excuses and stop making yourself believe in them. Whenever you make an excuse, you need to tell yourself that it is a lie, and you are going to make it no matter what.

# Chapter 25:

# Start Believing

How much do you believe in yourself right now? Then, what do you have right now in life? Everything you have in life right now shows how much you believe in yourself and believing in yourself will get you anywhere in life. In fact, most of us easily lose faith in ourselves when dealing with fear, setbacks, and failure. Not a few of them already gave up on their life goals as soon as they encountered their first setback. When you fail, it's natural to begin doubting your abilities and capabilities. But you need to remember that these failures are not the end of your journey toward success; you need to get back up again.

Believing in yourself is more important than the skills, training, or tools you have. It means that believing in yourself is the key to igniting your spirit toward self-improvement; you can't go anywhere without it. Having no trust in yourself will only sabotage you along the way in obvious or unconscious ways. Moreover, having a sense of self-doubt can influence others to pick up on that and not take you seriously. So, do you want to be your biggest cheerleader or your biggest critic? Indeed, you could choose either of them.

To start believing in yourself, you need to shift your focus to developing your strengths rather than your weaknesses. Once you've recognized your strengths, you should put more effort into areas you're already talented in to make you stand out from others.

When you strictly focus on developing your strengths, you will feel more competent and confident. Then, you need to communicate with yourself using positive self-talk. Positive communication can gradually develop new scripts in your mind that you are truly capable of doing anything (Tod et al., 2011). Moreover, you need to trust yourself by being honest and sticking to your word.

Self-reflection is essential to getting to the truth of what you feel, think, and need in life rather than focusing so much on what others want you to do. You should do what you believe is right by following your inner compassion. Once you've built trust in yourself, you will be able to make good decisions and achieve your goals effectively.

Other than yourself, you also need to assure that the people you spend time with are supportive of your goals, as they greatly impact your mindset and motivation. If you often feel negative and full of self-doubt when around certain people, you most likely happen to be around toxic people. Then, it's time for you to limit the time spent together with them and seek out another circle of people who can inspire and help you be your best self.

Another thing you need to remember is to celebrate your accomplishments, big or small, instead of being self-critical about them. To avoid being self-doubting again, you can always keep in mind what you've accomplished in the past and how well you've done it. Sometimes, reminiscing about your path gives you great motivation to seek another great accomplishment in the future. Thus, the need to watch your previous path will be the focus of the next challenge.

### *Challenge 25—Start Believing*

For this week's challenge, imagine yourself in the future, with your dreams coming true. Later, your future self will thank you for taking on this challenge. Then, for the extra challenge, you need to start believing by not doubting yourself anymore. You can find ways to work on your dream, step by step.

# Chapter 26:

# Watch Your Path

Hey there, have you realized that this is your 26th week of doing all these challenges? How well did you do with the previous challenges? Have you accomplished all of them? If not, how well are you doing? It's all too easy in life to focus on our only negative selves, with all their doubts and hesitations. However, looking at how well you're doing in life is a much more important aspect to consider. Sometimes, it's easier to say than to do, especially if we often blame ourselves for mistakes and compare our lives to others' accomplishments.

We often prefer to seek praise from others rather than noticing and loving ourselves for how wonderful we are. Others' compliments, on the other hand, are meaningless unless you first feel them within yourself. You need to love yourself first after all the challenges you've passed through. We are at challenge 26, which means 25 challenges are done. So, let's take this time to capture what we have been through so far. Give yourself credit for the bad habits you've broken, improved, and changed. Treasure these accomplishments, changes, and improvements in your life, understand that you can do it, and take off again!

We are often hard on ourselves to push ourselves to achieve success but being excessively hard on ourselves can only cause anxiety and hesitation to act as if you consider yourself a total failure. Thus, you can increase your drive toward positive changes in your life by giving yourself credit and practicing compassion with yourself, resulting in personal initiative and curiosity that takes you to greater and greater achievements (Breines and Chen, 2012).

It does not matter how small or big you think your progress is; notice and celebrate it. It takes you a while not to always compare yourself to others because we all get there in our own phases and timelines. Sometimes, it must be hard for us to acknowledge the little wins when we're still halfway there but taking the time to realize them can act as fuel to motivate you to move forward and further toward your dreams.

Looking back at the previous 25 challenges, you can remind yourself of the challenges you completely nailed or the ones you're most proud of completing. Keep in mind whatever gives you a feeling of pride and accomplishment.

Once you've watched and noticed all your improvements, you can now reflect on yourself and identify the things you'd change next time if you were to take this challenge again. Then, you can use these thoughts to be better prepared for future challenges. It's essential for us to also reflect on ourselves to see the whole picture of what happened during previous challenges. Thus, reflecting on us will be the focus of the next challenge.

### Challenge 26—Watch Your Path

For this week's challenge, you need to capture what you have changed and improved so far. Later, you'll discover that you're a better version of yourself than you were during the first week of the challenge. For the extra challenge, you should look back at your past before starting this journey, understand where you are now, and get ready for a bright future ahead!

# Chapter 27:

# Reflection

How often do you reflect on your strengths and weaknesses? What are your skills? What have you achieved? What could you do to possibly improve your weaknesses? Are you happy with all your accomplishments? If you've done a lot of self-reflection, you might know the answers to these questions. As its name suggests, self-reflection allows you to look into a mirror so you can assess yourself and gain a better understanding of yourself.

By using self-reflection, you can describe what you see in yourself objectively and be honest with yourself to get the whole picture of what happened, or why it happened, and how you can do it better next time. It's important for us to self-reflect in an objective manner because emotions often cloud our vision of what truly matters.

When we engage in subjective self-reflection, we begin to defend ourselves for our mistakes, which leads to us making excuses for our failures. Self-reflection assists you in responding to whatever situations arise in order to avoid doing things you may later regret.

When you do self-reflection, you can take the time necessary to consider the consequences of your actions and words to be most effective. Without self-reflection, we are going to live our lives without deeper thoughts while only juggling from one thing to another. Without self-reflection, we don't take time to step back and consider what valuable lessons we might learn along the way.

There is no actual right or wrong way to practice self-reflection, as everyone may express their thoughts differently, but you need to slowly incorporate this habit into your daily routine. A journal is a medium that is often used for self-reflection, consisting of important questions that you want to ask yourself.

These questions may vary from one person to another, but some of them can be about whether you are making the most of your time, whether you invest enough time to improve yourself, how well you react to things that happened this week, and whether you work your way toward success.

Once you've decided on questions to be included in the journal, you can release your thoughts there so you can occasionally reflect on your journey as you move forward. Before each self-reflection you do, you need to make a time when you can take a step back from the chaos of life. Then, you need to identify, honestly and objectively, what you feel and see based on your own perspective to answer these questions. Later, you can always refer to this journal to better identify, adjust, and improve the steps you need to take.

At first, you might find it difficult to be vulnerable in writing this journal, but you need to remember that self-reflection is a lifelong learning process. So, take your time and have fun with it! After you've finished your self-reflection, you'll have a better understanding of what you've accomplished thus far, your strengths and weaknesses, and areas where you need to improve. Then, it's time for you to start planning what you will do to achieve your goals effectively. Thus, planning your day will be the focus of the next challenge.

### Challenge 27—Reflection

For this week's challenge, you need to reflect on yourself at least once every day. You can think about the things you'd change next time if you can do it again. For an added challenge, think about yourself at least twice a day and write it down as a reminder to yourself.

# Chapter 28:

# Plan Your Day

We previously learned how to effectively measure our time per day and squeeze more time out. So, it's time to plan and fill your time as completely as possible so you don't waste any time. Keep in mind that we only have so much time each day. If you still feel that time gets away from you or keep wondering where all the time went at the end of the day, then you haven't planned your day well. Without proper planning, your goal of having a productive day is merely wishful thinking. You'll feel like 24 hours in a day will never be enough and end up feeling overwhelmed and disoriented. If you don't schedule your activities, you won't appreciate the time you have and will waste it.

Keep in mind that once you've lost time, you can never get it back. Once you've managed to plan your time well, you will take control of where you want to go, whether to cultivate a new habit, tame a never-ending workload, or learn new skills toward your goals. Not only is it helpful to schedule your day, but planning your day helps to decrease stress and give a sense of calm in both work and personal lives by prioritizing tasks to be done. Having this as an effortless habit allows you to become more productive and motivated throughout the day.

Planning your day is a habit where you can directly see the results right away, as you'll feel more organized, focused, and motivated with a plan. To start this challenge, it's important for you to at least have a general idea or priority of the tasks you need to get done the next day. Then, you need to decide on an approach to your daily planning that works best for you, whether to use a notebook, digital calendar, daily agenda, or even a to-do list app.

Writing your plans out will help you memorize and prioritize the tasks that need to be done immediately. To make this a habit, plan at the same time every day so that you will find it strange not to write it once. Brainstorming may be necessary to ensure that you've covered everything you need or want to do, such as upcoming deadlines, responding to emails, running errands, or attending appointments. You can do this brainstorming weekly to better review your daily plan.

To avoid overlapping work and life interests, you can group them in a separate list, so you'll get a balanced life. Not everything on your list must be a big project, you can list some quick tasks per day with a duration of 10–15 minutes, which can be squeezed in if you unexpectedly have spare time during the day. Later, you'll feel more satisfied as you check off a lot of those quick tasks and avoid procrastinating.

When you've made a daily to-do list, you need to frequently refer to it throughout the day. You should keep it at the top of your mind whenever you want to remember what you want to accomplish. Once you've already planned your day effectively, you'll realize that you have enough time to do more meaningful tasks. Then it's time to start noticing your worst habit, which frequently prevents you from progressing. Thus, eliminating your worst habit will be the focus of the next challenge.

### Challenge 28—Plan Your Day

To start this challenge, you need to plan the next day before you go to sleep about what you will do and how long it is supposed to take. For the extra challenge, you need to always stick to the plan and only make a minor adjustment every day.

# Chapter 29:

# Drop Your Worst Habit

Deep inside our minds and hearts, we all have a few terrible habits that are stopping us from going further. We must have been wishing that our terrible habit would go away, but it seems like we're absolutely stuck in a cycle of repeating those same behaviors over and over. Admit it or not, you already have some bad habits in mind that you want to drop as you're reading this. Is it spending way too much money on meaningless items? Is it always late on every occasion? Is it your inability to control emotions towards other people? Is it procrastinating when you have targets to meet? Is it watching too many series?

At one time in our lives, we must have tried to get rid of these habits at least once. Then, you often fail and feel worse than before as you can't resist the urge to continue the same habits. However, this vicious cycle is understandable because our brains become accustomed to doing these habits, potentially in the long run. But it doesn't mean we can't get rid of those bad habits; it just takes time, intent, and some effective behavioral changes.

To start dropping bad habits, you need to be honest with yourself. Sometimes, it's easy for us to ignore how some of our habits are limiting and blocking us from achieving our goals while worsening our health, relationships, finances, and even happiness. So being honest with yourself helps you understand what you're dealing with and how you can start making habit changes.

When you already know your bad habits, you need to cut out as many triggers as possible. Then, it'll be easier for you to eliminate those habits if you already avoid the things causing them. After that, you must plan for failure beforehand. It may sound counter-intuitive, but we all get off track every now and then, admit it or not. So rather than feeling guilty over that one mistake, plan to get back on track quicker and bounce back from the mistakes that you've been learning from the previous challenge.

When you've finished with the previous tips, you need to understand that the key to dropping a bad habit forever is to keep up your motivation. You should have compelling reasons for dropping that habit specifically. Then, you must tell yourself that reasons are constantly in your mind and give this some urgency by considering all the negative effects.

Once you've successfully dropped bad habits, now you need to replace them by adopting a good habit and making it part of your daily routine. Thus, picking up a good habit will be the focus of the next challenge.

### Challenge 29—Drop Your Worst Habit

For this week's challenge, you need to drop the worst habit this week that you've always wanted to get rid of. Listing your bad habits and their consequences will help you prioritize which one you want to drop most. For the extra challenge, you should drop two of those worst habits from the list.

# Chapter 30:

# Pick Up a Good Habit

Previously, we began to give up our bad habits for good. How well did you do it? Do you still do it every now and then? If it sounds familiar to you, maybe it's time to substitute good habits instead. Sometimes, the most effective strategy for dropping bad habits is swapping them for better ones.

Indeed, replacing bad habits is not a simple task, but it will be easier when you have a commitment and an unwavering desire to do it. Adopting better habits allows you to be healthier, whether mentally, physically, spiritually, or even financially. It allows you to explore something new while doing some research online about which one will fit your routine and interests.

To avoid feeling overwhelmed and anxious, you should only focus on one habit at a time. When that habit becomes an effortless routine, you can always move on to the next habit immediately. During this process, you should not only focus on the outcome. Most of us must only focus on the short-term result; instead, we need to focus on adapting the habit to our lifestyle.

To start this challenge, you must choose a good habit that you want to start with. Instead of forcing yourself with a totally new challenge, you can place a new habit that will work best in your already existing routine.

For example, you can start meditating or exercising if you are a morning person. If you're passionate about food, you can learn to cook. If you want to be in shape, you can learn to exercise regularly. In trying new habits, you learn that you know yourself better than anyone. Then, you need to control your environment to support the habit changes you want to make and avoid getting back into your old habit.

Besides the environment, you should be around like-minded individuals who can encourage you to stick with your new habit. At first, you may not get used to the new habit, so you can always use a reminder in the form of a visual schedule or phone alarm, as it takes time for an activity to turn into a habit.

Once you've failed to maintain your habit, you may tend to focus on the failure that led to negative self-talk. So, you need to keep in mind that it's okay to fail now and then; you just need to get up and try again. Stopping negative conversations in your head may already be your negative habit, so let's try to break that in the next challenge.

### Challenge 30—Pick Up a Good Habit

For this week's challenge, you need to pick up a good habit that will fit your existing routine well, so the process will be easier. For the extra challenge, you should pick up two good habits.

# Chapter 31:

# Stop Negative Self-Talking

Are you your own worst critic? How many times have you told yourself that you're a complete failure who can't do anything right? Or did you tell yourself that you'd never be successful in life like the others? Or even blaming yourself for things you didn't do? We've all probably heard these expressions when we are self-doubting, blaming, and judging ourselves.

At times, this little voice in our heads may keep us motivated during hard times. However, this voice can appear to be more harmful if you drown yourself in excessive negativity. Just like the law of attraction, negative thoughts will only bring negative outcomes.

If you find yourself having this self-talk all the time, these negative beliefs can greatly worsen your depression, decrease your self-esteem, and hold you back from success. If you're already aware of it, keep in mind that it's okay to deal with doubts and uncertainties in our lives, that is the essence of life—an unknown land when we try to explore more. Having negative self-talk will not help you in any way, and it never will. So why can't we find ways to make it possible rather than only bringing ourselves down.

To start this challenge, keep in mind that we can't stop those little voices inside our heads, but we can reframe the narrative of how we talk to ourselves. All of this to say, negative self-talk won't make you more aware of how to get things done better.

To stop this negative self-talk, you can start by noticing when you're being self-critical, so you can begin to stop when the exact thought chimes in. When you become aware of it, you need to replace those thoughts with something more positive and encouraging.

Shifting your attention to the bright side of a situation, no matter how small it is, may help you bring a positive light into your mind. Then, you need to train yourself to talk the way you'd speak to a loved one while giving empathy and encouragement along the way. By doing this, you need to ask yourself, "What would my parents say in these hard times?" or "How usually does my best friend give positive affirmation?"

If you've already done the previous steps, it's time to stop and refocus. Wherever your mind wanders to the worst scenarios ever, you can return to reality and focus on how you can improve, seek a solution, and make the situation all better. You need to rearrange your power to explore with determination while keeping on advancing to achieve your goals.

Once you've freed yourself from negative self-talk, you may find that previously you often complained about the things you couldn't control rather than doing something to make them better. Complaining, on the other hand, will not get you anywhere in life. Thus, the temptation to always complain needs to be totally removed from your mindset, which will be the focus of the next challenge.

### Challenge 31—Stop Negative Self-Talking

For this week's challenge, you need to stop the negative self-talk and cheer yourself up during hard times, instead. Later, you'll discover the effects of negative and positive self-talk on your self-esteem and progress toward success. For the extra challenge, figure out how to improve on the specific thing that lets you down.

# Chapter 32:

# Stop Complaining

Life is full of ups and downs. Indeed, adversity gets in our way without warning. When dealing with adversity, we all often complain about things to simply let the stress go. When dealing with hard times, it might be easier for us to complain rather than fix the root causes. It's normal to notice that we often dwell on and complain about things, but it can turn into a toxic mindset very fast. Some signs of one's complaining might be that you don't try to find a solution, experience a lot of regrets, and often feel irritable after complaining, leading to a feeling of hopelessness.

When you complain too much, you are getting your brain used to the habit of complaining, ending up in a vicious cycle. When you think and say negative things in the form of complaints, your attitude shifts to focusing only on negative things and feeling bitter. It surely takes a significant toll on your physical and mental well-being.

Whether it is your fault, someone else's fault, or simply an unlucky event, it doesn't matter. All you need to do is brush it off, learn what you can from it, take it positively, and treat it as a lesson. Then, thank life for giving you another lesson and use it as fuel to boost your journey toward success. When we can adapt to this mentality, nothing in life can bring us down. Remember, what doesn't kill you makes you stronger.

To start cultivating this mentality, you need to remind yourself that the actual constant thing in life changes, whether it's tomorrow, next week, or even next year. Even though you need to deal with hardships, a feeling of acceptance may greatly help you to positively adapt rather than only complaining about them. Change your perspective of adversity as an opportunity to learn rather than an impediment. Owning your own mistakes may help you be responsible for what life throws at you.

Complaining, on the other hand, will only make you blame others when, in some cases, you are the cause of the difficulty you are experiencing right now. Remember, all those things you complained a lot about are not forever, and this too shall pass. Spending your precious time complaining is an ultimate waste, so all you need to do is take the positivity and move forward while sufficiently learning from it.

Once you've cleared your mind of too much complaining, now it's time for you to better learn something new from the previous hardships you dealt with. Thus, learning something new will be the focus of the next challenge.

### Challenge 32—Stop Complaining

For this week's challenge, you must stop complaining by keeping in mind that every little thing happens for a reason. So, it's better for you to see the positive side of it rather than dwell on it and complain, which in fact can't change anything. For an added challenge, write down the lesson learned and find a positive side to it.

# Chapter 33:

# Learn Something New

When was the last time you let yourself learn something new? How did you feel after that? If you can't remember the last time, you learned something new, then it's time you start doing that again. Did you realize when we stop learning? We never stop learning! We continuously learn from school, college, workplace, life experiences, and even people around us. In this ever-changing world, we all must have felt left behind by others from all the knowledge that they have. Thus, learning something new is a great start to broaden your horizons to keep us relevant.

Besides, the practice of learning allows you to better understand yourself which can contribute to how you make life and career decisions. Learning also makes you a more adaptable person to keep up with trends and new skills leading to improved self-confidence. Another plus, our life will be more vibrant when we try to learn something new and discover what you're passionate about.

On the contrary, not learning new things can slow your brain down and make it less responsive. Meanwhile, learning rewires and strengthens the brain contributing to reducing the risk of dementia and Alzheimer's (Sterling, 2017). As the brain learns, neurons relay information faster and more efficiently which further improves your ability to do something new (Stevens, 2014).

If you don't know what to learn yet, you can try looking at things you're most curious about or a long-neglected hobby from the past. Later, you'll discover immeasurable satisfaction in learning, regardless of age or career choice, if you find your meaning in it.

When you've already made up your mind, you can seek out more opportunities to practice the skill set. The more practice you have, the more likely you are to succeed at accomplishing your goals. Then, you can seek out additional resources in the form of a book, online learning courses, or even a community center to help you overcome learning obstacles.

As you learn new skills, you may likely make a mistake. So, you need to treat these mistakes as a beneficial tool for better and more effective learning in the future. Even if you discover that the acquired skill does not suit you, you can always learn about another skill or ability.

Consider your life as a journey of learning and discovering new skills every day. Then, do not let yourself have any "0" days, which means that you don't even improve yourself by even 1% in life. Thus, motivating you to not have "0" days anymore will be the focus of the next challenge.

## *Challenge 33—Learn Something New*

For this week's challenge, you need to learn something, whether it is cooking, reading a book on new topics, or studying a new course. Whatever it is, pick something new. Then, for the extra challenge, you need to always remind yourself not to quit. Later, you can always strive for new things along the way, and don't be discouraged if something doesn't suit you well.

# Chapter 34:

# No More "0" Days

How far has the progress toward your goals been lately? Do you feel like making slow progress? If you have no idea how well you progress toward your goals, it's time for you to notice your daily progress, however small it may be. Don't only focus on bigger improvements! Often, we do not notice when something has changed or improved until it does. But if we look closely at it, we can see how the gradual process turns into bigger changes.

In fact, we do not transform overnight because it takes days, months, or even years of hard work and commitment. Thus, we need to start improving ourselves day by day, even by as little as 1%. Even if you only feel like improving by 1% per day, it's still better than having "0" days.

No matter what you do, be better than "yesterday you". Without realizing it, most of the dreams that we had ended due to a long period of inactivity rather than because we gave up. Thus, we need to develop a growth mindset while pursuing meaningful goals.

A growth mindset encourages continuous self-evaluation, skill development, and the search for new opportunities to learn and develop throughout life. Our progress towards a goal can also increase our positive emotions and overall enhanced well-being, leading to increased motivation to act (Pychyl, 2008). So why don't we utilize this link just to get started?

To start making progress toward your goals, you need to establish compelling reasons and an emotional connection to what you really want in life in your career, relationship, health, finances, academics, or personal life. When you have already made up your mind, you tend to establish motivation to move forward. Then, you should develop your tangible goals and timeline to better enable you to track your changes.

It helps you remember why, how, and when you want to make those life changes.

When starting the first step, you need to keep in mind that the changes can't be made overnight. At first, you may feel like you're still far away from your goals. Thus, you need to focus on the gain and not on the gap. When you look too closely at the gap, it makes you only focus on the future without treasuring what's happening in the present.

By starting with seemingly small progress, you are successfully building one on top of another until it becomes visible to others. It's better for you to achieve your small increment daily. During the progress-making process, it's important to practice self-reflection and evaluate the strategies you've already adopted. Ask yourself what other things you can improve and prevent new obstacles.

Regular self-reflection improves how you better function in the future and keeps your goals constantly in mind. It's also essential to celebrate small wins throughout your progress, which better provides you motivation to continue by pampering yourself, preparing a special meal, or taking a weekend getaway.

Once you've made progress, there must be a moment where you want to quit, so don't attempt to do it. Thus, it's essential to just hang on to those quitting moments in life, which will be the focus of the next challenge.

### Challenge 34—No More "0" Days

For this week's challenge, you need to be better than "yesterday you" in career, health, finance, academics, relationships, or personal development. Whatever you try to achieve, remember that progress is important no matter how far you are from your goal. For the extra challenge, you must challenge yourself and push yourself further.

# Chapter 35:

# Hang On

Previously, we've challenged ourselves with continuously making progress, but another thing to be anticipated is a critical moment when you want to quit. In life, we've dealt with these exact same moments. How did you react to it? Did you really quiet or hang on to it? When you're pursuing, these moments are inevitable and often make us think, "This is harder than I thought," "No matter how much I tried, I'm going nowhere," or "I am a total failure." If this sounds familiar, keep in mind that every excitement and enthusiasm you have for your goals will be followed by discouragement and despair.

Whenever you want to quit, you need to emphasize the importance of progress rather than the result alone. Remember, these pains are temporary and necessary. Without pain, we can't become stronger. The moment that you want to quit is an opportunity for you to overcome yourself and conquer the emotion. It doesn't matter whether we like it or not; hanging in there is the only way we have. Overnight success is a myth, always.

To hang on to hard times in life, you need to adopt the "I won't quit" mindset, no matter what. Think about persistence when things get tough, focusing on finding a solution, and remember that setbacks are only temporary. Then, getting inspired and motivated while watching someone else persevere toward success in books, movies, or biographies may help you get there on your own.

Moreover, remembering your earlier motivation for achieving that goal will help you stick with it during difficult times. If necessary, you can add more reasons to strive for that specific goal, making it more important for you to achieve. The more meaningful and compelling the reasons you have, the more likely you are to not quit halfway.

When you've already found your "why", you need to find your "how" by shifting to a different approach to accomplishing your goals. If you feel that you've failed to do the previous strategy, you can always seek another strategy and practice it until you find something that does work. Instead of seeing these tough times as an excuse to quit, you should consider them as steppingstones toward your goals. Then, push yourself harder while taking consistent action to achieve your goals.

Even if you haven't seen the immediate result yet, keep chipping away till you make it. Hanging on to ourselves is the most important thing to keep in mind, as you are the one who is responsible for your own happiness and hardships, so stop asking for others' favors. Hence, being on your own is an important topic to be discussed in the next challenge.

### Challenge 35—Hang On

While making progress in life, you need to anticipate the desire to quit that comes out of nowhere. So, for this week's challenge, you need to hang on to it whenever quitting moments happen. For the extra challenge, you need to push yourself further to finish it well.

# Chapter 36:

# On Your Own

No doubt, having a supportive circle of friends and family is important to provide love, compassion, and insight. However, knowing that you can do anything on your own requires independence and self-reliance. We must stop being at ease in a safe environment and learn to rely on no one.

How can we know if we're being self-dependent on others? If you have a problem, did you ask for others' favor in the decision-making process? Did you often ask for help even though you knew that you could do it alone? Did you feel like you were depending on others' presence, support, or companionship throughout your personal development? Be honest with yourself; you need to promote being on your own if you're familiar with these situations.

Being self-sufficient takes a lot of effort, persistence, and time, but it is truly rewarding to see yourself feel safer as you have all the resources and confidence to handle pretty much any circumstance the world offers. Being self-sufficient allows you to feel happy about yourself, in yourself, and by yourself without needing to rely on others. This mindset and skill are essential to have as we grow older and learn to live independently.

There are things in life that we must figure out for ourselves. We must go through them on our own. There is a territory where you cannot rely on anyone, so get used to not relying on anyone; be as self-sufficient as possible!

If you want to develop self-reliance inside of you, you can start by noticing and treasuring your strengths in your career, relationship, financial, and personal lives. While doing this, it's essential for you to reflect on your previous accomplishments. As a result, it will boost your confidence without needing others' validation in the form of compliments and praise. You can already feel secure and worthy of love.

Once you are already confident in your strengths and accomplishments, you'll find yourself not asking for others' guidance anymore when solving problems and making crucial decisions. Keep in mind that you can handle any circumstance in a way that we feel secure about.

Whenever hardships get in your way, remember that you own your choices and actions, so it's your responsibility to fix things up. Moreover, you need to resist the urge to immediately ask others to clean up your mess and meddle with it. If you have issues expressing negative emotions, you should find healthier ways to do so instead of venting to others.

Once we've mastered this mindset, we will never be in doubt while always feeling sure of ourselves, regardless of multiple failures in the past. Indeed, taking ownership of whatever, you do is important, as you take full responsibility for the possible consequences. Thus, taking ownership of whatever, you do will be the focus of the next challenge.

### Challenge 36—On Your Own

For this week's challenge, you need to do all your needs by yourself and totally stop asking for a favor, if feasible. You need to figure everything out on your own. For the extra challenge, you can't ask for any help at all, not even from your family.

# Chapter 37:

# Take Ownership

We have all experienced good and bad things. Whenever good things happen, we almost instantly praise ourselves for causing them to happen. But we've rarely admitted and instead, blamed others for causing this to happen whenever bad things happened. Ultimately, this tendency makes us feel powerless about something that happened in our life rather than admitting and taking ownership of the decision we've made before causing everything to happen. Think about every time we say, "I am overweight because of my genes", "I'll never get a promotion because my boss hates me", "I'm always late because the traffic is bad" or "Life is unfair; I never get good things in my life".

When we often use these phrases, it expresses a lack of personal responsibility for the circumstances in life by shifting the focus of problems onto other people and the unfairness of life in general. While it may feel easy to blame others, it slowly saps your power and leaves you feeling helpless and anxious all the time.

When you shift away from your proper responsibility and ownership, you now lack the ability to take charge of your own personal life, which impacts your career, relationships, and overall happiness. We have more control over our lives than we think we do. Indeed, taking ownership and responsibility for our actions and decisions can feel challenging. It includes our willingness to learn from mistakes, a sense of owning both our successes and failures, and a stop to blaming others for our own circumstances.

Taking control of your life, on the other hand, is truly rewarding and liberating because you can choose how to respond to certain circumstances with accountability and fortitude. It empowers you to realize you have a new level of consciousness where you're able to make a choice.

Taking ownership is one way to find out who we are and how good we are at doing something. When you own it, you will do it at your best. As a result, you will provide the highest quality and work the hardest on it because you know your name will be on it. Until we take ownership of our lives, we are still being avoidant and letting the external factors of life determine what we do, think, and feel.

To start regaining control over your life, you need to notice whenever you begin to blame others and refuse to own your fault. Oftentimes, this tendency has become an automatic response, so you need to spot it whenever you try complaining when an unfortunate situation arises. If it happens, you must immediately pause and reassess your way of thinking by asking yourself, "What's my role in this incident?" "What can I learn?" and "What's the bigger picture of this?" Then, try to come up with solutions and ways to make this right.

Instead of aiming for a perfect solution right away, this brainstorming allows you to improve creative thinking, problem-solving skills, and a sense of control over your problems. By practicing this, you will also be able to develop a sense of personal responsibility and develop conscious decision-making.

When you hold yourself accountable to others, you are more likely to own your own thoughts, decisions, and actions. As a result, this will increase your sense of responsibility toward yourself.

Once you've taken ownership of your life, it's also important to own your mistakes and forget about them, but make sure to learn from them. Forgetting your mistakes is an essential mindset to ensure you're not stuck, which will be further discussed in the next challenge.

### Challenge 37—Take Ownership

For this week's challenge, you need to take ownership of whatever you do by taking full responsibility without pointing fingers. Then if you mess it up, you must fix it, no matter what. If you don't know, learn how to!

# Chapter 38:

# Forget Your Mistake

We all make mistakes in our lives; we are imperfect because we are humans, not robots. Nothing beats the feeling of complete defeat and despair that comes from making mistakes in life. It easily makes us total failures in our own lives. No matter how small or big our mistakes are, these feelings seem to come along and weigh heavily on our mental health.

Do you still remember mistakes you made in the past? How does that feel right now, in the present? If you still have these regrets over past mistakes, it's time for you to forget these mistakes before they slowly consume us. These intense regrets can only burden your life moving forward and impede happiness, affecting your physical and psychological well-being (Newall et al., 2009). Thus, you need to keep reminding yourself that you are so much more than your past mistakes. We learn from mistakes rather than becoming stuck in them.

To start reframing your view of past mistakes, you need to process your emotions and give yourself some time to accept them. Before you're in the acceptance phase, take some time to grieve the regrets holding you hostage. Then, we have no choice but to accept that what's done is done and think of the options left. This can be accomplished by accepting responsibility for what has already occurred, expressing regret for your mistakes, and forgiving yourself.

Even though you may not be able to undo the past, making improvements for the future might help you forgive yourself and move on without dwelling on the past. Then, think about the silver lining: either we gained a new understanding of life or people around us, became more mature, or even ultimately brought us to another source of joy. There is always a silver lining.

When we've understood the silver lining and accepted those mistakes, we can use them as experiences to guide us in a more positive direction toward our goals. Then, rather than focusing solely on the mistakes, decide what is most important to you now and in the future.

Remember, it's okay to let go of your mistakes and breathe. Next time, make sure to learn from and grow from your mistakes in order to be better than before. That's what truly matters. Once we've overcome our mistakes, now's your time to shine brighter than ever. Just do whatever you want to do, and don't overthink the past or the future! Further, practicing a great start will be the focus of the next challenge.

## Challenge 38—Forget Your Mistake

For this week's challenge, you need to forget whatever mistake you make, but make sure to learn from it well. Don't let the mistake bring you down; take it as a process and a good experience to have. For the extra challenge, you need to analyze why and where everything went wrong, then figure out how you can do it better next time.

# Chapter 39:

# Just Do It

Think about the last time you told yourself "Just do it" and did it. How often do you do it? Or are you still overthinking whenever you want to start something? Imagine how far behind we are because of that overthinking inside our heads. We always intend to do this and that but never follow through. Think about how many times we are blocking ourselves by overthinking. When you keep overthinking about the same things or worry about things you can't control, leading to hesitation to start, it won't take you anywhere, and instead, it will take a toll on your mental health.

Is it all worth it in comparison to the missed opportunities and goals? Of course, not every idea in your mind will work, but at least it allows you to explore and test things out rather than only overthinking and imagining how things turn out. Remember, the only beneficial overthinking is the one that leads to action.

Don't wait for inspiration or momentum to get started on those ideas! Just do it! If you can get yourself to start, you'll find that you can keep going. Just like a snowball gathering speed, sometimes motivation and momentum build after we begin.

Overthinking can easily become ingrained in your behavior in ways that you aren't even aware of. You should be aware whenever overthinking kicks in and realize that it isn't helpful at all. Whenever you have an idea, just simply start it without the need to weigh the pros and cons, as sometimes that can hold you back from even starting. Whatever big or small steps you take, momentum will soon keep you rolling to produce improvements over time.

Starting the initial action makes it easier for you to continue, no matter how far you are from the actual goal you want. The initial action may appear minor, but it represents a significant step forward in your overall process toward your goals. Now, all you need to do is find out what makes you stop, make strict routines to avoid procrastination, and build rituals that make you feel good.

Besides, you should create a routine around your goals to enhance the power of momentum. Then, maintain this routine until you accomplish your goal. We need the momentum to do things; pair your action with your mind—they are the perfect match! Once you've decided to just do it, you need to trust your vision of yourself in the future and keep working towards it. Thus, trusting your vision will be the focus of the next challenge.

### Challenge 39—Just Do It

For this week's challenge, you need to do it as it appears in your mind. Whatever is on your mind, do not overthink; start it right away!

# Chapter 40:

# Trust Your Vision

How many times do you have a vision and end up not executing it at all? Why haven't you executed it? Oftentimes, we care so much about others' opinions that it makes us hesitant to even start the journey to achieve our vision. That's why you shouldn't listen to them at all, especially when they dismiss your ability to realize your vision. Hold on to your dreams no matter how far you've strayed from them!

Trust the vision in your heart and soul about what you want to be, what you see yourself doing in the future, and what you are willing to do to achieve them. Then, you need to believe in them, make a positive intention around them, and start creating those visions into reality without anyone else's voice buzzing in your ear.

When you've already had visions in your head, it's a great start to improving your future. Keep in mind that you can achieve your vision if you're willing to act with faith in yourself. Consider how you wished you were where you are now years ago. It is the same; we just must repeat it!

If your visions are still blurry to you, then you are most likely not spending enough time to define what success really looks like. You can write out those visions as many times as necessary until you have a clear vision. Throughout this brainstorming process, you'll later find motivation within that clear vision.

When you've already made up your mind, place it somewhere you often see it, either on the bedroom wall, next to your computer, or as your phone wallpaper. Then, let yourself soak up that written vision and believe it passionately, which allows you to have a sense of purpose, dedication, and endurance throughout your striving for those visions.

When your visions appear overwhelming, break them down into small steps of accomplishment so you can complete them step by step. Then, you need to have a strong commitment toward your vision, as it's needed to always help you get back up and start over again whenever tough times happen.

When the vision is clear and the belief is strong, action becomes a pleasure rather than a chore. Throughout your striving for your visions, you need to understand that success won't happen overnight, so you must be patient if your process is steady. Thus, being patient during the process toward your vision will be the focus of the next challenge.

### Challenge 40—Trust Your Vision

For this week's challenge, you need to keep working toward your vision. Keep in mind that achieving those visions takes time and dedication. You must believe in yourself because you are the only one who determines what life gives you.

# Chapter 41:

# Patience

Can you wait for a buffering icon or a slower internet connection? Can you stand late people getting in your way? Can you resist the urge to lay on your horn when the traffic light just turned green? If you can relate well to these situations, then you may not be a particularly patient person. In this fast-changing world, don't we all tend to be very goal-oriented and want to see a fast and almost immediate result?

Being patient is never really a thing, as we often want everything done in a heartbeat. Admittedly, this feeling of impatience leads to a great deal of wasted energy, exhaustion, and unnecessary stress. Whereas good things in life can't be rushed as it takes time to properly develop. A seed needs time to be a fully grown plant. A wound needs time to heal itself. It also takes a lot of time to feel content and secure about your accomplishments in your personal and professional lives. The result you always want is not an overnight miracle' it's all about the process.

Do not give up because you cannot see the result yet and be patient with yourself. One step at a time, eventually we will all get there. No matter how far from it we are, if we keep advancing, we will surely get there! Being patient means that you need to control your responses to things that may not meet your anticipated expectations.

While being patient and letting go of pressure, we will be able to see the big picture and focus on the journey itself. The more room we make for the journey, the transformation will be more effective, and we can better embrace the growth we have right now.

To start being patient, you need to realize that every little good thing in life takes time. Remember how you take many things for granted; being patient will make you cherish and treasure each good thing that happens. Then, you need to commit to learning in the process. Take time to slow down while learning something new every day throughout the process.

Moreover, you need to understand that the process can still progress. Even if the result appears invisible to you, every day, progress is inching forward towards your goals below the surface. Enjoy where you are right now so you don't miss out on the growth and potential that are possible in the process.

Learning to be patient, like anything else in life, takes practice and time. You must give yourself time to get used to being patient with even the tiniest discomfort getting in your way while being grateful for what life gives you now.

This change surely won't be easy, but you'll accomplish whatever you've set your mind and heart out to do with calm and controlled perseverance rather than always being in a rush and impatient. Moreover, meditation is an effective way to help you bring peace to your mind and better manage your thoughts, especially in the hustle and bustle of everyday life. Thus, practicing meditation in our routine will be further discussed in the next challenge.

### Challenge 41—Patience

For this week's challenge, you need to be patient with yourself and be rather focused on the process. Remember that progress means steadily moving forward.

# Chapter 42:

# Meditation

We are crowded with too many things in life, from real-life people in work or personal life to the rise of social media. Given the numerous distractions and unnecessary flows of entertainment or information, an effective method for properly gathering all our thoughts and refocusing on ourselves is desperately needed. But how much time do we make and spend on ourselves every day? How often do we sit down quietly and listen to ourselves?

Previously, we've been practicing how we can measure our time and get the most out of our limited time per day. Meditation is one of the beneficial habits that we can adapt to our routine. Meditation allows us to take a break, reset, and manage our minds from the hustle and bustle of everyday life.

Although we cannot eliminate our daily stressors, meditation can provide the mental shift required to deal with constant change and uncertain times ahead. It may take some time to establish a meditation routine and reap the most benefits out of it, but eventually, you'll be living a healthier life physically, mentally, and spiritually.

Overall, practicing regular meditation in our routine can increase our level of anxiety and depression. It is also proven that there are structural and functional brain changes from a long-term meditation practice (Behan, 2020). As our focus and clarity improve during meditation, you'll find it easier to make decisions and complete tasks because you already cope with your distracted mind. Besides, you'll appear to be in a calmer state of mind whenever dealing with discomfort.

Meditation is a low-cost and simple way to release and contemplate inner tensions, contrary to popular belief. All you need to do is provide a relaxed and quiet location with few distractions while focusing on an open attitude and paying attention. There is no actual right or wrong to practicing meditation, which can be adjusted to fit your preference and personality. Even a few minutes will have a great impact. If you're a beginner, you can start with 5–10 minutes and gradually increase it as you get more comfortable with it.

Before meditating, it's essential to find a place to sit quietly and make sure your sitting posture is stable. Then, take deep breaths through your nose and follow the sensation of your breath going in and out. If you notice your focus and mind wandering, don't be easily discouraged, as it's common to happen at first, and just simply return your attention to the breath. You can set an alarm to track your meditation time.

Whenever you feel like finishing the meditation, gently close your eyes and take a moment to feel your environment. Later, you'll notice changes in how your body feels and the thoughts or emotions inside of you. Meditation allows you to better appreciate and focus on the present moment. Sometimes, taking a step back and enjoying quality time in the moment is much needed for us to be grateful, so it'll be further discussed in the next challenge.

### Challenge 42—Meditation

For this week's challenge, you need to meditate for 15 minutes before bed to ensure you can disconnect with the world and have a restful sleep. For the extra challenge, you need to meditate when you wake up as well. Later, you'll be in a better frame of mind to face the day.

# Chapter 43:

# Quality Time

The craziness of life can be so draining and exhausting at times that it completely distracts you from the joy that surrounds you. How often did you find yourself thinking about what happened yesterday or what might happen tomorrow? How often do you worry about them rather than living and focusing on what is happening in the present? How does this feeling affect your life?

Sure, you'll most likely feel anxious and stressed as your mind and body go separate ways, even though you may not realize it. This tendency to dwell in the past and worry about the future can leave you worn out and feeling out of control of yourself. Not only does it rob you of the enjoyment of today but choosing to live in the past or the future robs you of truly living.

The only way to keep your body and mind in sync is to be consciously aware of what's going on and concentrate on the present. You've probably heard a lot of people around you give similar advice about not getting caught up in the past or future, being present in life, or not letting the present moments slip away easily. However, these pieces of advice are easier said than done, as there are many things that we must often anticipate. Indeed, we need to force ourselves to live in the present moment to better treasure what truly matters.

To be consciously aware of your surroundings and live in the present doesn't mean that we can't dream about the future. You can still be able to think about both the past and the future in small doses to better identify where you've gone wrong in the past and to have just long enough to prepare for your dream.

By living in the moment, all you need to do is stay in the present moment for most of the day. No matter how much you think about the past and future, the moment you experience right now is where you have actual control over it. Then, it's essential to turn off the TV, computer, or phone to better wind up and savor the present.

Oftentimes, we consciously let technology take over our lives instead of being mindful of what's happening around us. We should notice the world around us, even the smallest things, and be thankful for them to help us cultivate more positive experiences in the present. The key to living in the moment is to not worry much about tomorrow. Each second you wasted worrying about tomorrow is a second of the present wasted. Instead, focusing on ways to deal with existing issues and how to improve the current moment will help you a lot more. Life now flies fast—don't miss it.

Once you've lived in the moment and have quality time in the present, it'll help you to observe experiences and people around us, better and more closely. By observing our surroundings, you'll find there are a lot of things you can learn from other people. Thus, learning from life through observation of surroundings will be further discussed in the next challenge.

### *Challenge 43—Quality Time*

For this week's challenge, you need to focus on the moment without thinking of something else, whether enjoying the environment, listening to others, or pulling your mind back into the scene. For the extra challenge, you also must treasure and savor these moments.

# Chapter 44:

# Learn from Lives

When you think about learning to improve your life, you are most likely to think about how you can learn from books, biographies, motivational podcasts, or even movies. But have you realized that you can learn anything in life from the people around you? From the very moment we are born, don't you realize that your parents, relatives, and close friends are the ones who provide you with learning experiences?

There is always something we can learn from people. Always. Thus, taking a closer look, observing, and paying attention to details about them may be the most effective way to learn. Learning from others' lives might seem easy for you, but it requires a lot of commitment to see things in the bigger picture.

When you learn from others, you'll understand the choices they make and the consequences of them. Seeing others' mistakes teaches you to avoid falling into the same trap while deciding to make a different choice that you think might work better.

Meanwhile, seeing others' success most likely makes you decide on the same choice while inheriting their knowledge and emotional wisdom from the decision-making process. This makes learning from others' successes and mistakes appear to be more efficient than figuring this out on our own.

Learning from others allows you to avoid learning things the hard way as much as possible. Learning things, yourself takes a lot of time and numerous efforts. It is also mentally draining, especially without a definite result. It doesn't mean we have to tally to avoid any potential risk, though, because that will only set you back to taking actual action.

Learning from others can minimize the chance of failure while continuing to take risks. All you need to do is learn just enough to start acting and keep learning throughout the process. Once you have mastered this, you can read people's attitudes and characteristics like a book. Keep in mind that observational learning doesn't mean we have to simply copy others' decisions and actions. Instead, observational learning incorporates your own motivation and goals as you seek to engage in or avoid specific behaviors.

To start learning from others, you need to have intrinsic motivation and a curious mindset to learn well while remaining focused. Then, you can simply observe and stay aware of what they do to receive certain rewards or values. You can also initiate a conversation with them to gain a better understanding of their values and motivations.

Once you've learned from others, now it's time for you to reflect on your own strengths and weaknesses. That's how you can decide whether to imitate or avoid their behavior to better minimize the potential risks in the future. It also makes you more receptive to advice and criticism from others. Being open and safe enough to share your emotions is a much-needed mindset to have, as it helps you not get easily overwhelmed by the situation, which will be discussed in the next challenge.

### Challenge 44—Learn from Lives

For this week's challenge, you need to observe people around you and learn something from them. Later, you'll be surprised at how much you can learn from them. Then, if possible, you need to pay attention to the details and the reasons behind every action or decision they make.

# Chapter 45:

# Share Your Emotion

Being vulnerable and willing to share our emotions are not easy challenges to overcome. It may seem easy when we are having happy feelings, but it means another thing when it comes to struggling times. Though it seems impossible and awkward at first, being open to other people can truly make your already heavy load lighter. You are the one who needs to learn how to share your feelings.

We, as humans, have limited space within us, just like a cup. If the cup is already full, how can you pour it without spilling? Think about one time you burst into tears when dealing with even a small inconvenience; how you were so easily irritated; or even how you were being sarcastic to mask your fear of being vulnerable. Eventually, something must come out before the cup is spilled. Everywhere and to everyone.

No matter how hard you try to make negative emotions disappear, they won't just evaporate into thin air. Instead of constantly filling the glass, why not let some out and make room for newer ones, which may or may not be positive? Facing those emotions head-on by sharing them with a trusted friend, family member, or even a therapist is the most effective strategy to deal with whatever's going on in your mind. Furthermore, putting negative emotions into words and sharing them with other people helps us regulate negative experiences, which results in reducing emotional distress (Lieberman et al., 2007).

When starting to open about your emotions, you need to allow yourself to accept that your feelings are valid. Oftentimes, we are hesitant to share our emotions with others because we think that they aren't valid or worthy of being shared. Imagine how we always think, "This is my own problem, and I don't need to share any of this with others." This kind of mindset will only bubble up until one day it explodes.

Once you've realized these emotions are valid, you should share them with your loved one(s), such as a friend, family member, or significant other, who can help you feel better understood and supported. These people can help you gain new perspectives or even more objective points of view to analyze the situation you're struggling with.

Remember, don't expect other people to understand whatever is on your plate now; they aren't mind readers! Then, opening to others can bring you back to the present and get you back on your feet again, so you'll be more motivated to do something about these feelings. Later, you can find out that the existence of others can truly help you through tough times. Then, now it's your turn to act as a "provider" who can understand, support, and take care of others just like they've done to you.

To take care of others, you need to understand that it's not always about you, so how to feel and be aware of that will be discussed in the next challenge.

### Challenge 45 – Share Your Emotion

To begin this challenge, you must share your emotions with someone you can trust. Then, for the extra challenge, you should express yourself and unwrap the emotion, even if it's something you've felt inside for the longest time.

# Chapter 46:

# Take Care of Others

Previously, we've learned how to share our emotions with others so we can feel more understood and supported while dealing with hard times. You can now understand what they meant by ups and downs. So, have you taken care of your loved ones the same way? We can't expect others to always be the ones who give without also giving to them. The world doesn't revolve around you. We must learn how to become providers just because we can and can do so.

Remember, you don't need to become rich or a social worker first to be able to take care of others; just be yourself. Also, it only takes a minute or even a second to let your loved ones know that they are supported and valued by you. You can say that you love all your loved ones sincerely, but if you don't spend enough attention, thoughts, and actions on them, you simply don't truly care. Your loved ones cannot feel your feelings for them unless they see it in your actions. So, use your actions to care. When you see the beauty of taking care of others well, you won't realize that you will become addicted to it.

To start taking care of others, you need to have a mindset where you give care because you truly care about them, not because you expect them to do the same or because you think you "should" do that. Then, you can start by transforming your love for them into actual action, no matter how simple it seems.

Simple acts of kindness are often overlooked in everyday life, but they have a greater impact on others. Whenever it is, you should ask them how they are and show them that you genuinely want to know their feelings. Then, just listen to them; don't shift the focus on yourself. Whenever they initiate a sharing moment, this isn't about you; it's only about them.

When they've done sharing their emotions, it's your time to validate their feelings and assure them that you can empathize with their situation. Your presence already means a lot to them by directing your full attention to them and receiving them as they are, espccially through tough times. You may not be able to provide them with a meaningful solution, but that's fine. Instead, you can still act in comforting ways and do much-need practical tasks for them that they'll find helpful. Seek other ways to offer help and comfort to them.

While taking care of others, it's also essential for you to not neglect your own needs to be supported and valued. You can't help others if you don't accept yourself completely, flaws and all. So, it's time for you to be aware and get ready to face your weakness by being honest with yourself, which will be further discussed in the next challenge.

### Challenge 46—Take Care of Others

For this week's challenge, you need to listen to others rather than focus on yourself and talk about yourself. Show how you truly and sincerely take care of them. Then, for the extra challenge, you must give them the support they need in any form you can provide.

# Chapter 47:

# Face Your Weaknesses

Let's face it, we all have weaknesses because we are mere humans. Some of us can be aware of our weaknesses while trying to overcome them. Meanwhile, some others ignore their weaknesses and pretend they don't exist, which continues to hold us back. Whereas, neglecting our own weaknesses prevents us from achieving our full potential, leading us to feel less than others, ashamed, and weak.

Neglecting your weaknesses only leads to a whole other set of issues. Instead, dealing with and facing your weaknesses head-on allows you to improve self-acceptance and cultivate self-awareness, which can free you from self-deprecating thoughts. When you are aware of your weaknesses, you allow yourself to accept every part of you that makes you unique as a person.

Self-acceptance of your weaknesses greatly helps you feel better in your own skin because you've already accepted the things you struggle with as part of who you are. While being self-aware of who you are with all your weaknesses and strengths may make you seem like a confident person to others, you want to be vulnerable rather than pretending you don't have a weakness.

Being brave enough to confront your weaknesses pushes your self-deprecating thoughts away. Think about how often you have said, "I'm worthless because of my weaknesses" or "I can't handle anything well in my life" previously. We all deserve kindness, especially from ourselves.

To start facing and overcoming your weaknesses, you need to be honest with yourself and be able to write down every weakness you have. It can be challenging and daunting at first, but keep in mind that this will only push you forward. If it's hard to start, you can begin by listing unfavorable outcomes in your life, which can better direct you to clearly see your weaknesses. If you can't admit your weaknesses, objectively see yourself, and accept who you are right now, you will never improve in life.

Remember, having weaknesses does not signify that we have missing pieces in us. However, it serves as a reminder that we all have some darker and brighter sides to our personalities. Once you've made a list of your weaknesses and accepted yourself as who you are, you need to reflect on how you want things to change for you to be a better version of yourself. Then, you need to work toward strengthening your areas of weakness.

Developing a solid action plan with a timeline will help you improve yourself. Throughout your journey to overcome weaknesses, remember that it won't be easy because it's all about being vulnerable to reveal your fears and things that make you self-doubting. It's all about change, an unavoidable and frightening change. But you don't have an option except to improve yourself and stick with your action plan, which will be discussed in the next challenge.

### Challenge 47—Face Your Weaknesses

For this week's challenge, you need to write down all your weaknesses. Think about how you couldn't finish some tasks in the past or what skills you were supposed to have but didn't have in your career, academic career, or personal life. Then, for the extra challenge, remember you don't have to hide or lie about your weaknesses. It's only you; just be honest with yourself.

# Chapter 48:

# Plans to Improve

Previously, we made a list of your weaknesses and accepted them as part of who you are. Now, it's time to tackle your assignments one by one with a solid plan. Don't be afraid of stepping out of your comfort zone; changes are inevitable. A "comfort zone" is a dangerous place to be, as it most likely makes you stagnant and never finds growth. Thus, only facing and understanding your weaknesses is not enough; you also need to improve them with the plan you specifically tailor for yourself. Don't let your flaws and failures define who you are and how you live your life. Thus, a solid plan to improve yourself is a much-needed scheme to keep you on track.

A self-development plan allows you to have a clear perspective on what kind of person you want to be, what skills you need to have, and what accomplishments you want to achieve. When you already have those in mind, you can map out your short- and long-term goals and set the timeline. These plans and timelines give your life a better sense of purpose and meaning, keeping you motivated to achieve your goals while tackling your weaknesses. No matter how long it takes, stay in the fight.

To start designing a solid plan, you need to be in the right mindset first, seeing your weaknesses as a challenge to be improved on rather than as a chore to be done. Then, you must focus on defining your goals, which need to be realistic and straightforward. Having a concrete goal creates a sense of accountability, so you can better figure out the actions to get there. The more precise your goals are, the easier it is to estimate the timeline later.

When you've already made a list of your goals, you need to prioritize them based on their urgency and importance to you. Then, you're ready to set milestones on your self-improvement journey to push you harder and further to achieve your goals. Now, it's time to design an action plan consisting of actions that you intend to take to accomplish your goals. Whatever your goals are, you need to be determined to be consistent with them. You may not see the immediate results, but it surely makes you more resilient as time goes on.

Feel free to modify the plan later if you feel like you are not making visible progress while being non-critical about it. What matters is that you try to begin. Once you've initiated the first step, you can measure the progress and efficiency of your action plan. Later, you'll find yourself already exceeding your existing limit. Doesn't it feel good to exceed your limit? Thus, breaking through your limits will be discussed in the next challenge.

## *Challenge 48—Plans to Improve*

For this week's challenge, you need to come up with plans on how to improve yourself based on what you wrote down in the last challenge. Use this challenge to reflect on what you want to accomplish and how you will achieve it. For the extra challenge, you must make sure you execute your plans step-by-step within the timeline.

# Chapter 49:

# Exceed Your Limit

How do you feel right now after completing the previous challenges? Have you already felt like going beyond your limit? How does it feel when you realize your improvement? If you feel like you haven't improved much toward your limit, then it's time to get yourself out of the cocoon you've built around yourself. When you believe that you still have a limit, it'll act as a false image of having limited potential, which prevents you from becoming what you are capable of. As a result, this mindset can transform into fear, doubt, or a mental block leading to giving up even before trying.

Life, on the other hand, provides you with an infinite number of opportunities and possibilities to grow and become the best version of yourself at any given time. Do you want to be mediocre, just like where you are now? Can you guarantee that you won't regret it in the future and only wish you had done something before?

If you don't want to be filled with regrets in the future, you must dare yourself to stretch your own boundaries and take the leap of faith to know how far you could've gone. Remind yourself that the limit you have right now is self-imposed and based on what you choose to believe. So, it's not your reality; it's all primarily in your mind. Don't let those limits define who you are; push them back a little each moment of your life and fly higher!

To begin exceeding your limit, you need to develop a can-do mindset, which is essential as the first step to getting out of your comfort zone and breaking free from a mediocre life. This mindset acts as fuel to help you chase your dreams. Then, finding compelling motivation can also help you push your existing boundaries.

No goal is impossible if you are already fired up from within. Ask yourself: What things excite you the most about accomplishing your goals? Also, don't only chase what you know. It means that you need to take on newer and progressively more difficult challenges. Embracing much harder and unknown challenges makes you used to being outside your comfort zone, which is a better situation to strive for better achievements in life.

To better motivate yourself, you need to take some time to vividly visualize where you want to go. This can be done by looking at how others have already reached where you want to go. Then, use these to inspire you to also reach your goals. So now is the time to go for it rather than keep putting it off.

Once you've got compelling reasons and a vivid visualization of your goals, waste no time procrastinating and strive for them right away. Don't stop yourself until exhaustion because your fight is endless! Strike for excellence instead of perfection! Nobody is perfect, and neither are you. Thus, striving for perfection will only hold you back, so seeing that nobody is perfect will be the focus of the next challenge.

## Challenge 49—Exceed Your Limit

For this week's challenge, you need to write down what you've improved so far and how you have changed. List all your accomplishments throughout these challenges. For the extra challenge, you must understand that you can do it better and cheer for yourself in the future.

# Chapter 50:

# Nobody is Perfect

All these challenges have come to an end to ensure that we can improve ourselves in a positive and rather excited mindset. How well did you do with all the previous challenges? If you've made a few mistakes throughout these challenges, that's totally okay. Don't be too hard on yourself! Nobody is perfect; accept it as a fact. Perfectionism is an impossibly high standard with no room for imperfections that we all can't fulfill. Perfectionists inside our heads will often see mistakes as evidence of our inferiority to others.

Being a perfectionist makes us expect that we must know everything, to outperform everyone, to never make the tiniest mistake, or to never let anyone down. Thus, pursuing only perfection in life adds so much stress and so many burdens to our already demanding lives. It mainly affects our relationships with others, as we often see ourselves as total failures.

Moreover, perfectionism increases social anxiety and depression and even increases vulnerability to obsessive-compulsive disorder and eating disorders (Egan et al., 2011). So, it's essential to remind ourselves that nobody is perfect. Strive for excellence, not perfection. Stop only focusing on what is missing, how you still can't reach the result, and the fact that you're still working toward your goals. Instead, you need to focus on how much progress you've made and when your strength will increase your ability to move forward.

When we are striving for excellence, we can see that mistakes are inevitable, so just deal with them and value what we can learn from them. Rather than pursuing only perfection, pursuing excellence promotes a better view of personal growth and improvement based on our mistakes. Pursuing excellence is a balanced mindset where we maintain our high standards and accomplishments while maintaining our self-care, excitement, and relationships with others.

To start letting go of some of the perfectionism in our minds, we need to shift our view of mistakes and failure along the way as the only way to get us closer to our goals. Making a few mistakes here and there allows you to learn better and be more progressive. Striving to learn more, act more, and improve more on everyday progress is better than only pursuing perfection, which often holds us back. We need to enjoy the journey and progress ourselves while celebrating any accomplishments we've made along the way.

To better overcome perfectionism, we should become aware of when our mind tends to do it. Then, take some time to pause, rest, and shift the focus to the progress itself. Besides, we should make a conscious effort to focus on the positives, as focusing only on the negatives will only lead to perfection. Moreover, allow yourself to make mistakes and see how well you can slowly manage your feelings toward those mistakes. Afterall, making mistakes here and there isn't that bad, right?

Remember, we should be kind to ourselves and practice self-acceptance to keep us motivated. Monitoring how things influence your perfectionism may help you shift away from it, including social media, motivational podcasts, TV, or even books, which are often packed with the culture of hustling.

Once you've shifted from the temptation of perfectionism, doesn't it feel good to not be too hard on yourself? Giving yourself credit for whatever accomplishments you've made is much more important, which can be further discussed in the next challenge.

### Challenge 50—Nobody is Perfect

For this week's challenge, you need to accept imperfection(s) throughout your life. Striving for only perfection in life holds us back from making continuous progress, which is far more important than only being perfect.

# Chapter 51:

# Applause

With these past 50 challenges, I hope you all improved yourself and broke through the limitations that you originally had. You certainly did well with all your effort. So, it's time for you to give yourself credit, remember the moment and the feeling, take the positivity, and keep moving forward. Being harsh to yourself is essential to growth, but we also need to understand the importance of giving ourselves credit. How often do you criticize yourself for not getting much done? Have you noticed that you are hard on yourself if things don't go right?

No matter what your goals are, being hard on yourself only stresses you more in this competitive world, leading to giving up easily. Indeed, it's easy to get wrapped up in things we haven't accomplished yet. So, you need to pay better attention and measure your progress more objectively. Then, you can be better at giving yourself credit for the numerous great things you've made. Giving yourself credit can help you achieve more and greater accomplishments by promoting self-confidence, self-love, and self-compassion.

Giving yourself credit for your accomplishments does not absolve you of responsibility for your setbacks. It's all about letting go of the past while focusing on the positive and developing a positive mindset. This concept motivates you to give better and more appropriate thanks, no matter how small a step you take toward your goals.

You need to be your own cheerleader to cultivate the mindset that you are worthy, competent, and deserving of all the love from yourself and others. It's better to not rely on others to validate your own success. Enjoy your own company through the ups and downs!

To initiate this mindset, you need to make time for as little as 5–10 minutes a day to pat yourself on the back and look back on things you've accomplished, even the small ones. Cheer yourself on as you finish a big presentation at work. Have a nice meal after your chores. Do some self-care routines after stressful times. Do what makes you happy and excited about it! Even if things didn't go as planned, allow yourself to celebrate and acknowledge the fact that you've tried it before.

This mindset and all the celebrations you've made help you realize that you want to achieve and check off many more accomplishments. These changes may not happen overnight, so you need to consciously practice them from time to time. Later, you'll notice how positive your mind and mood are at the end of the day, even after bad ones.

### Challenge 51—Applause

For this week's challenge, all you need to do is sit back, give yourself a round of applause, and enjoy the results from the previous 50 challenges. Savor the positivity around you and use it as fuel to keep moving forward.

# Chapter 52:

# Take Care!

What a journey!

Life is tough, but whatever goals you want, they will wait for you at the top. It is always difficult to walk to the top of the mountain. But once you are there, the view will not disappoint you. Life is still worth living and is packed with the meaning of learning to reveal who we really are. Even though life is hard, it's still beautiful if you have a positive mindset. Even in adversity, get back up and keep going while viewing it as only fertilizer to help us grow and become stronger.

Indeed, life is tough, but so are you. In various circumstances in life, we might often ask ourselves, "Why is my life hard?" Think about how you are not alone because more and more people have already successfully overcome similar challenges that you are currently facing. If they can, you can do it too—even better!

Believe that there is always a solution out there waiting to be discovered. Whatever life throws at you, just believe there is something that makes it worthwhile. Whenever you decide to stop and settle in your comfort zone, you should ask yourself whether you can bear the burden of never reaching your full potential. Besides, are you ready to only wonder if there is a better life than the one you've lived up to now?

Every day, you only have two choices: either live the life you've lived now or live the life you've wanted forever while embarking on never-ending battles with yourself. Settling with the first choice may sound safe at first, but it won't take you anywhere in life.

Meanwhile, brace yourself with the second choice and change the fact that you are meant to do more than survive. Whereas I believe that we all can achieve more than we've already accomplished right now. Don't settle for less! Just have strong faith in yourself and believe that everything happens for a reason.

## Challenge 52—Take Care!

We've finished these challenges well, through ups and possibly more downs. But we've made it! I wish you all a very bright future. Keep breaking through and take care!

# Conclusion

Yay! We've made it and still stand strong after the past 52 challenges. Do you think that this is the end of the challenge? Unfortunately, it is only the beginning of our journey toward continuous improvement of our mentality and attitude through life's ups and downs.

Remember that living in a constantly changing world necessitates effective adaptation; YOU are your best ally. So don't hold on for dear life, but rather embrace the ride. I hope this book can be a handy guide for you, especially to lead you step-by-step toward the best version of yourself and the accomplishments you've never had before. You want things you've never had before, so you also must do something you've never done before.

This book challenges you in many ways you've never experienced before. After you've read and embarked on all these challenges, you'll realize that even the smallest habit you've done previously can result in a significant change within the challenge of not hitting the snooze, not scrolling, keeping your place tidy, not using your phone, and shopping only for what you need.

When you've completed these seemingly insignificant challenges, don't you feel like they build up and create a snowball effect that encourages you to undertake more and more challenges, leading to everlasting routines?

Further, there are various challenges that require and emphasize how we can manage our already limited time efficiently within the challenges of measuring your time, planning your day, no more "0" days, making quality time, and many more similar challenges.

After these challenges, don't you realize that you've had better performance and less stress throughout the day? Also, this book emphasizes how we need to take control of our own lives within the challenge of being on our own, take ownership, trust our vision, drop the victim mentality, and plan to improve.

Furthermore, pushing us out of our comfort zones is a necessary skill set for learning how to be comfortable with being uncomfortable as a result of the challenge of getting uncomfortable, staying away from what we love, taking a different angle, and just doing it. Overall, these challenges require us to push ourselves on a self-improvement journey.

No excuse, just do it!

If you've already felt perfect about yourself, especially after being done with these, unfortunately, you are wrong. Nobody is perfect. There is always so much room to make improvements because everyone can learn something new any time and everywhere. All we need to do is be better every day than we were yesterday.

Once you've practiced it, you'll seek more and more experience to explore new ideas and perspectives. Who knows that we might find out a different version—and yet a better version—of who we are now? So, it's always welcome for you to read this book repeatedly, as these challenges may have different understandings and interpretations at different times.

There is always another level out there waiting for them to discover; there is no end to improving ourselves.

See you on another level!

# References

Behan C. (2020). The benefits of meditation and mindfulness practices during times of crisis such as COVID-19. *Irish journal of psychological medicine*, 37(4), 256-258. https://doi.org/10.1017%2Fipm.2020.38

Breines, J. G. & Chen, S. (2012). Self-Compassion Increases Self-Improvement Motivation. *Personality and Social Psychology Bulletin*, 38(9). https://doi.org/10.1177/0146167212445599

Deffler, S. A., Leary, M. R. & Hoyle, R. H. (2016). Knowing what you know: Intellectual humility and judgments of recognition memory. *Personality and Individual Differences*, (96), 255–259. http://dx.doi.org/10.1016/j.paid.2016.03.016

De-Sola Gutiérrez, J., de Fonseca, F. R., & Rubio, G. (2016). Cell-Phone Addiction: *A Review. Frontiers in Psychiatry*, 7. https://doi.org/10.3389/fpsyt.2016.00175

Egan S. J., Wade, T. D. & Shafran, R. (2011). Perfectionism as a transdiagnostic process: a clinical review. *Clinical Psychology Review*, 31(2):203-12. https://doi.org/10.1016/j.cpr.2010.04.009

Fuhrman, J. (2018). The Hidden Dangers of Fast and Processed Food. American *Journal of Lifestyle Medicine*, 12(5), 375-381. https://doi.org/10.1177/1559827618766483

Hill, T. (2019, March 25). *Is Addiction a Choice?* Mental Health First Aid from National Council for Mental Wellbeing. https://www.mentalhealthfirstaid.org/external/2019/03/is-addiction-a-choice/

Kets de Vries, M. F.R. (2012). Are You a Victim of the Victim Syndrome? *INSEAD Working Paper* No. 2012/70/EFE. http://dx.doi.org/10.2139/ssrn.2116238

Li, Z. & Zhang, J. (2012). Coping Skills, Mental Disorders, and Suicide Among Rural Youths in China. *The Journal of Nervous and Mental Disease*, (10), 85-90. https://doi.org/10.1097/nmd.0b013e31826b6ecc

Lieberman, M. D., Eisenberger, N. I., Crockett, M. J., Tom, S. M., Pfeifer, J. H. & Way, B. M. (2007). Putting feelings into words: affect labeling disrupts amygdala activity in response to affective stimuli. *Psychological Science*, 18(5), 421-8. https://doi.org/10.1111/j.1467-9280.2007.01916.x

Mateo, R., Hernández, J. R., Jaca, C. & Blazsek, S. (2013). Effects of tidy/messy work environment on human accuracy. *Management Decision*, (51), 1861-1877. https://doi.org/10.1108/MD-02-2013-0084

Mattingly, S. M., Martinez, G., Young, J., Cain, M. K. & Striegel, A. (2022). Snoozing: an examination of a common method of waking. *Sleep Research Society*, 45(10). https://doi.org/10.1093/sleep/zsac184

Newall, N. E., Chipperfield, J. G., Daniels, L. M., Hladkyj, S. & Perry, R. P. (2009). Regret in Later Life: Exploring Relationships between Regret Frequency, Secondary Interpretive Control Beliefs, and Health in Older Individuals. *The International Journal of Aging and Human Development,* 68(4). https://doi.org/10.2190/AG.68.4.a

Pychyl, T. A. (2008, June 7). *Goal Progress and Happiness.* Psychology Today. https://www.psychologytoday.com/intl/blog/dont-delay/200806/goal-progress-and-happiness

Rai, J. (2021, April 2). *Why You Should Stop Checking Your Phone in The Morning (And What to Do Instead)*. Forbes. https://www.forbes.com/sites/forbescoachescouncil/2021/04/02/why-you-should-stop-checking-your-phone-in-the-morning-and-what-to-do-instead/?sh=13a93eb42684

Rentfrow, P. J., Goldberg, L. R., & Zilca, R. (2011). Listening, Watching, and Reading: The Structure and Correlates of Entertainment Preferences. *Journal of personality*, 79(2), 223. https://doi.org/10.1111%2Fj.1467-6494.2010.00662.x

SecurEnvoy. (2012, February 16). *66% of the population suffer from Nomophobia the fear of being without their phone*. SecurEnvoy. https://securenvoy.com/blog/66-population-suffer-nomophobia-fear-being-without-their-phone-2/

Sterling, C. (2017, July 25). *What Happens to Your Brain When You Learn a New Skill?* Continuing Education on Central Connecticut State University. https://ce.ccsu.edu/what-happens-to-your-brain-when-you-learn-a-new-skill/

Stevens, A. P. (2014, September 2). *Learning rewires the brain*. Science News Explores. https://www.snexplores.org/article/learning-rewires-brain

Tod, D., Hardy, J. & Oliver, E. (2011). Effects of self-talk: a systematic review. *Journal of Sport and Exercise Physchology*, 33(5), 666-87. doi: 10.1123/jsep.33.5.666.

Worley, S. L. (2018). The Extraordinary Importance of Sleep: The Detrimental Effects of Inadequate Sleep on Health and Public Safety Drive an Explosion of Sleep Research. *Pharmacy and Therapeutics*, 43(12), 758-763. https://doi.org/https://www.ncbi.nlm.nih.gov/pmc/articles/PMC6281147/

Made in the USA
Las Vegas, NV
11 April 2023

70485225R00066